Race Track Attack Guide

Laguna Seca

The Enthusiast's Approach to the High Performance Driving Experience on America's Road Racing Courses

Edwin Reeser, III

Sericin Publishing Company

Copyright 2010, Sericin Publishing Company

All rights reserved. World rights reserved. No part of this book may be reproduced in any form or by any means, electronic or mechanical, including photocopying, recording or by any information storage and retrieval system, without the prior written permission of Sericin Publishing Company, except in the case of brief passages embodied in critical reviews or articles.

ISBN Number: 978-0-9841724-0-5

Library of Congress Control Number: 2010905116

DISCLAIMER: The contents of this book are true to the best knowledge of the author. All recommendations are made without guarantee on the part of the author or the publisher. The author and the publisher disclaim any liability incurred in connection with the use of any data or recommendations in this book. In particular, no portion of this book should be taken to suggest or condone the violation of any traffic laws or the practice of any unsafe driving.

Printed in the United States of America

Track photos taken by Ed Reeser.
All maps used to illustrate the Laguna Seca racing lines are from Matthew Reeser and Kathryn Marcellino.
Cover photo - "The Corkscrew"- Edwin Reeser

A publication of Sericin Publishing Company,
Sericin Management, LLC.
Matthew Reeser, Editor in Chief

Contents

Foreword 5
Introduction 7
Perspective 11
Track Entry 19
The Entry 23
Merge 25
Turn 1 31
Turn 2, the "Andretti Hairpin" 39
Turn 3 47
Turn 4 51
Turn 5 57
Prepare for the Unexpected 63
Turn 6 71
Turn 7, the "Rahal Straight" 77
Turn 8, the "Corkscrew" 81
Turn 9, the "Rainey Curve" 87
Turn 10 91
Turn 11 93
Track Exit 95
Distinguishing Characteristics 97
Conclusion 99
Closing Note on Driving Lines 101
Track Checklist 103
Tech Inspection Form 107
Dedication 109
Acknowledgement 111
About the Author 112

Foreword

Having worked with Ed Reeser at Nissan Sport magazine, I know how keen he is for detail. While most of us stumble through motorsports and life (those two inseparable endeavors) relying on our meager talents, Ed is constantly on the lookout for the smallest details. When he turns his attention to each racetrack, his ability to analyze the topography of the circuit, together with his explanation as to *why* each detail is important can be more valuable than gold.

Perhaps just as important is the display of a thinking man's approach to motorsports. In my twenty-odd years of being an active racer, I've witnessed just how critical this aspect of driving has become. Beyond purely technological aides such as state-of-the-art data acquisition, each participant can get the most out of their track day experience by flexing that most important muscle—the one located between their ears—before, during and after the event. And as you read about balancing risk vs. reward through each corner of the track, you'll begin to appreciate Ed's successful approach to high-performance driving.

Beyond that, and even if you use this book to gain greater insight into specific corners or areas of the track you are having difficulty with, Ed offers side notes and suggestions that are well-worth paying attention to. Most of us have learned these lessons through years of bent fenders, busted wheels or worse. I'd suggest reading and re-reading his descriptions slowly to give yourself time to assimilate this information. Once you hit the track, things will happen quickly and you will be faced with making split second decisions that could impact (pun intended) your ability to continue a pleasant day.

Finally, Ed makes the point that no tangible rewards (trophies, points or money) are part of a typical track day or HPDE. But I disagree. The reward that each successful participant takes home at the end of the day is the beautiful, shining car of your dreams. Hopefully, the same one you drove to the track in! And beyond this, it's my belief that each successful lap—driven to the limit of our abilities—transforms us as individuals. Making us more aware of the capabilities of our vehicles and what we can and cannot do, is a priceless experience. Have a great day at the track!

David Muramoto
Editor-in-chief
Nissan Sport Magazine

Laguna Seca Raceway

Introduction

Laguna Seca Raceway is located on State Highway 68 approximately ten miles west of the City of Salinas, California, at Highway 101 and ten miles east of the City of Monterey, at Highway 1. Initially constructed in 1957, the road course has undergone several extensions and layout modifications since then, and presently is an eleven turn 2.238 mile configuration.

This Track Attack analysis will present the driver with a tool to help prepare for a high performance driving lap at the famed Laguna Seca Raceway, including track entry and track exit procedure.

While we should always do a track map study of a circuit before driving a course, a two dimensional map, in car video, video game simulation or still photos of this track do not adequately convey the 300 foot elevation change that climbs steeply from the entry to Turn 5 to the highest point on the course at the hill crest entry to Turn 8, followed by the plunge down hill from Turn 8 through the "Corkscrew", the dramatic "roller coaster" sweeping drop of the Rainey Curve and descent into Turn 10.

A short straight burst out of Turn 10 is followed by a supermarket aisle wide 125 degree low speed left at Turn 11 into the front straight, accelerating up the hill at the start/finish line, through the full throttle hill crest kink at Turn 1, then steeply downhill into and through the Andretti Hairpin of Turn 2 that finishes the descent on corner exit to the bottom of the road course.

The thrill, excitement and challenge of driving this course are world class. And under the proper supervision, accessible to most drivers at this time.

The Track

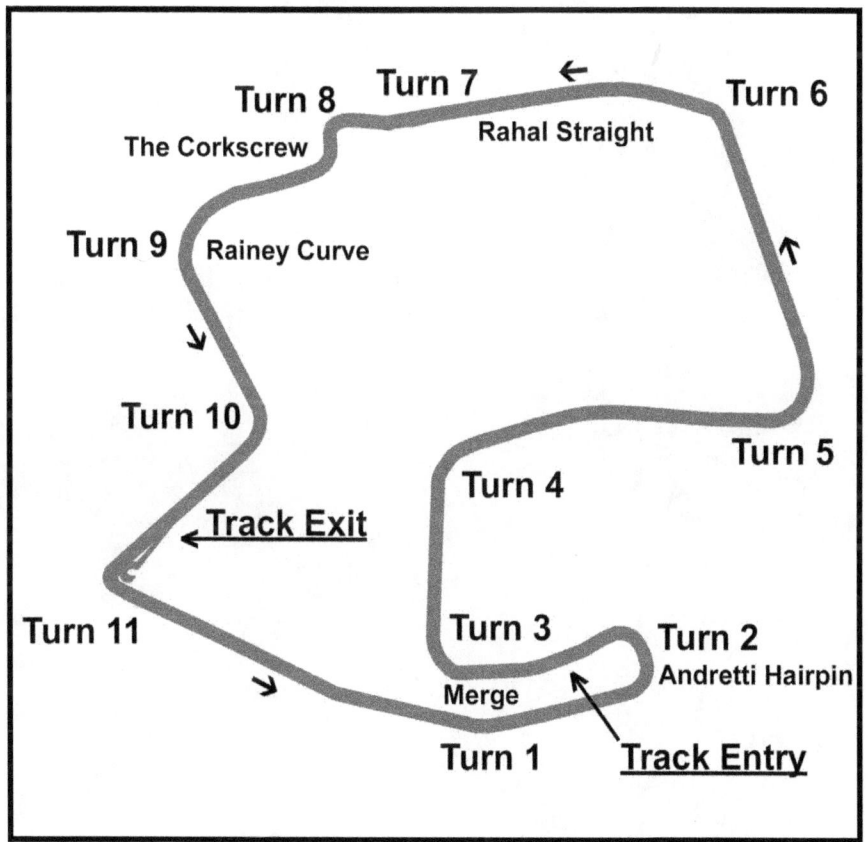

Perspective

Reality Check: Before we get into how to enjoy High Performance Driving Education ("HPDE") and the track notes for Laguna Seca, a few words about what this experience is about and its risks.

Many sports involve highly developed skills where you throw, catch, strike, or kick a ball. If you make a mistake the result typically involves a lost point, a change in possession, a replay, or perhaps a lost ball and a "do over" with a scoring penalty, and the game continues. *In high performance driving, you are the ball, and there are no second chances.* Accordingly, driving the "ball" over the fence or into the lake is not an option.

Some sports have a significant potential of serious injury or death if things go wrong. You may do everything right yourself, and still get caught by the mistakes of others or unpredictable events. Mountain and free climbing, scuba diving, sky diving, spelunking, bungee jumping, hang gliding, bull fighting and driving a car, motorcycle or bicycle fast all can have seriously negative consequences, irrespective of fault. If introducing even a moment of inattention to a relatively safer activity, such as crossing a street on foot, can be fatal, (stepping into the path of a bus while reading the morning paper, for example) then it is clear that a moment of inattention in one of the aforementioned activities is potentially more so.

All sports require a detailed level of knowledge and practice to perform well. Striking a golf ball is not an inherently natural series of coordinated actions. Neither is throwing, catching or hitting a baseball, climbing the face of a rock wall, or making a controlled sky diving free fall. HPDE driving is most definitely an undertaking that benefits from serious study of the geometry of tracks, the components and working of your car, the art of driving, safety considerations at all levels, and physical and mental preparation of the driver. You will drive better and be safer if you devote the time and energy to do it right by studying, and practice.

Driving a car is an inherently dangerous activity. Driving a car fast, even under the best of conditions and preparation in a well-controlled track situation, is even more so. A 3000 pound car moving at 60 mph has the potential energy to move a 5,808 TON block of concrete one foot. That car moving at 120 mph has the energy to move a 23,232 TON block of concrete one foot. A speed of 120 mph is not really "fast" in the auto racing world. There are numerous circuits where a street car can reach speeds of as much as 150 mph, or more. As kinetic energy increases as the square of speed, twice as fast means four times the energy. If there is a problem on the street or the track, all that energy has to go someplace before your car comes to a stop. If it is dissipated through braking to a smooth stop it is highly desirable, as contrasted with a series of violent roll over strikes upon the ground or against a concrete wall. This is especially true if the concrete wall does not move and the energy is absorbed by the compression of the car with _you_ inside of it.

As you spend more time on the track, the odds of having an unpleasant experience will tend to catch up with you. You will exit the track surface, lose control of your car or have someone lose control of their car in front of you. All people make errors in judgment. All things mechanical and electrical can and eventually will break or fail. Random events can and do suddenly occur. They have happened to me, and all of the other drivers that I know, so there is no reasonable expectation that you will escape this fundamental reality any more than you can defy the laws of gravity.

But you can prepare to make the best of it when bad things happen. Part of the focus of this book is to bring to light how you approach driving and maintaining your car, and whether you may need to consider changing your approach to make yourself a safer driver on the street and track. You may find that track experience can benefit you on the street, keep you out of trouble. Not because you can drive faster than others, but because you are more aware, have developed additional car control skills, and can get the most out of your car and yourself in an emergency.

If you cannot accept the responsibility or consequences of driving on a race track, don't do it. Driving a car under the laws applicable in all licensing jurisdictions that I am aware of is not a right, it is a privilege, and you are responsible to do everything you reasonably can to prevent damage to your car, the cars of others and/or injury to yourself or others. That is just for street use of a car. On a track, the safety and preparation expectations and requirements of most sponsoring organizations is even higher, and the assumptions of the risk that you take for your actions, and those of others, is higher as well. Nobody is forcing you to drive on the track, and certainly you should not allow anybody to persuade you to do it. Thoroughly investigate and study first, and then make up your own mind.

Once you have made the decision that you are going to drive a car on a race track, then it is your responsibility to do it as safely and intelligently as you can, for your own sake and that of those around you. Such care includes your careful preparation of the car, its transport to and from the track, and staging in the garage and pits. It includes your personal skill development and preparation through driving schools and practice in car control on and off the track. It also includes how you enter the track, how you leave the track at the end of your session, how you evaluate the risk areas of the track and develop your plans to deal with those risks.

Be mentally, emotionally and physically prepared for the stresses. The level of concentration required is more intense and sustained than any driving experience you have had on the street, and possibly more than any other experience you have ever had anywhere. The faster you go, the more data you have to deal with, and the less time and distance to deal with it, and however good you think you are, or actually are, sooner or later you will find you are not good enough at some point, in some corner, on some day. That is not good or bad. It is just the way it is.

While you cannot eliminate all of the risks associated with high performance driving, you can do a lot to reduce and to manage risks by proper preparation of yourself and your car, attention to safety at all levels of equipment and driving techniques, and by running with reputable organizations and sponsors of track day events. Please do all of that and more.

The satisfaction that comes from driving a very fast lap derives from an assembly of many little things. It takes time, practice and study to get it right, and patience is a virtue. Fast driving does not come from deciding that you want to drive "fast" and stepping harder on the gas and brake pedals of a car with a big engine. Rather it comes from developing the car control and driving skills to accelerate, turn, brake, shift and balance weight on the car **smoothly and precisely** under a wide array of differing conditions and circumstances. As you improve those skills... speeds increase, lap times decrease, and more importantly your errors should decrease. Slow is *smooth*, and smooth becomes *fast*.

What defines "fast" is what is fast for you. Compared to a horse, you will be going very fast, and for a turtle... even more so. Yet for a beam of light or radio wave you will be virtually stationary! As to other drivers... don't get trapped into that element of competition. It is of no importance that somebody else in a different car is a few seconds slower or faster than you.

If you want to be competitive against others in your driving, and there are many people who do, there are organizations that arrange competitions for "time attack" or racing against the clock versus other drivers, as well as the traditional and popular "wheel to wheel" racing. Those are not HPDE and should not be confused with HPDE. If you want to do that type of competitive driving, get yourself into a proper racing organization and follow their program

In HPDE, there is no blood, honor or money on the table. No fashion beauties with bouquets of flowers, no gigantic bottles of champagne to spray adoring fans, no poster sized checks for amazing sums of money, await you for being the fastest driver on the track.

The goal is to learn to drive as skillfully as you can as safely as you can at speeds within the capabilities of yourself, the car, and the track under the specific conditions of the day, and then go home at day's end with car and body unscathed.

Do not be dismissive of the repeated emphasis in this analysis on high speed issues associated with this circuit, as the purpose is to help you know where to focus to manage that speed. Going fast, and going fast *safely,* are not the same thing. Any person, and many trained animals, can get behind the wheel of a powerful car, hold the wheel straight and put the accelerator to the floor. You must not mistake the capabilities engineered into the car to be an extension of your capabilities as a driver, especially with respect to car control at speed.

Having a fast car and being a fast driver are two unrelated statements of fact.

Know your limitations. Driving this course is terrific fun, but you must recognize and respect the limitations of the track, the car, and yourself with clarity. While most beginners approach track days with the reserve and caution appropriate to reduce risk of mishap, there is perhaps a greater risk on this track for the intermediate and advanced drivers who are pushing the envelope of performance limits for their cars, and their own driving skills, but at higher speeds than they may be used to. Control recovery at high speed is more difficult, and the consequences of lost control to man and machine more severe, so respect this attribute of speed when driving Laguna Seca, where corners that are technically simple at slower speeds like 6, 9 and 10 develop subtle nuances at higher speeds that can surprise the driver.

Track Entry

Safety for both the entering driver and the drivers already on the track is a priority for every road course and participant. Every track has a unique set of issues associated with its track entry and its track exit. You need to study and understand both track entry and track exit procedure and technique before you show up. Given the high speeds at Laguna Seca on the front straight, the close proximity of cars on track to those entering the track at the hill crest corner apex of Turn 1, the potential difficulty for the car entering the track to visually pick up on track cars approaching Turn 2, and the merger or "blend" of the driving lines of entering cars and on track cars approaching Turn 3, special attention must be paid to this aspect of driving the Laguna Seca course.

Track Entry begins from the extreme left, with the starter stationed below the bridge at the start/finish line and separated from the "hot pit" lane by a concrete k rail wall on the right, which hot pit lane is itself separated from the main track by another concrete k rail wall farther to the right.

TRACK GUIDE - LAGUNA SECA

Drivers will grid their cars in either single or double file format at the starting grid at the direction of the starter. Drivers are typically called to the grid for their driving session ten minutes before the scheduled start, and should all be present by not later than three minutes before the scheduled start.

The starter or assistant starter should check wrist bands to confirm that all drivers on the grid are in the proper session group and qualified to participate in that session, and to pass along any last minute information ("there was a coolant leak at the right edge of the track surface on exit from Turn 6. It has been wiped and sanded, but still may be a little slick so be careful there").

While you are on the start grid, cars may come and go from the hot pit lane to your right from the current session on track. The track entry lane and hot pit lanes merge immediately after the start, and are then separated from the main track surface by the k rail for only a few yards past the start/finish line, at which point the only thing then separating the entry lane from the main track is a pair of narrowly separated parallel white painted lines.

Upon receiving direct release from the grid by the starter, the entering car must stay well left of the painted lines up and beyond the crest of the hill through the corner apex of Turn 1, after which the entry lane physically separates from the main track surface down hill to the inside of the Turn 2 Andretti Hairpin, curls hard left inside of that corner, and blends the entering car into the **left** edge of the track surface at the corner exit for Turn 2, where the cars on the main track are on the **right** edge of the track surface from corner exit and track out from Turn 2.

With respect to the actual point of entry on the track, Laguna Seca has as safe an entry as any road course designed. Speeds are moderate, and both entering and on track cars have time and space to see each other, and if necessary to make adjustments. And they are oriented at opposite sides of the track surface. However, every track has at least one point where the driving line of the entering cars and the driving line of the on track cars "blend" together, and this is a primary risk point, though not necessarily the only one. *There are two points of risk for potential intersection by entering cars with cars on the main track at Laguna Seca that both the entering cars and cars on track must pay careful attention to.*

Entry lane. *Note separation from track by two white lines. Entering car should stay well left of the left most painted line until the entry lane is physically separate from the main track.*

The Entry

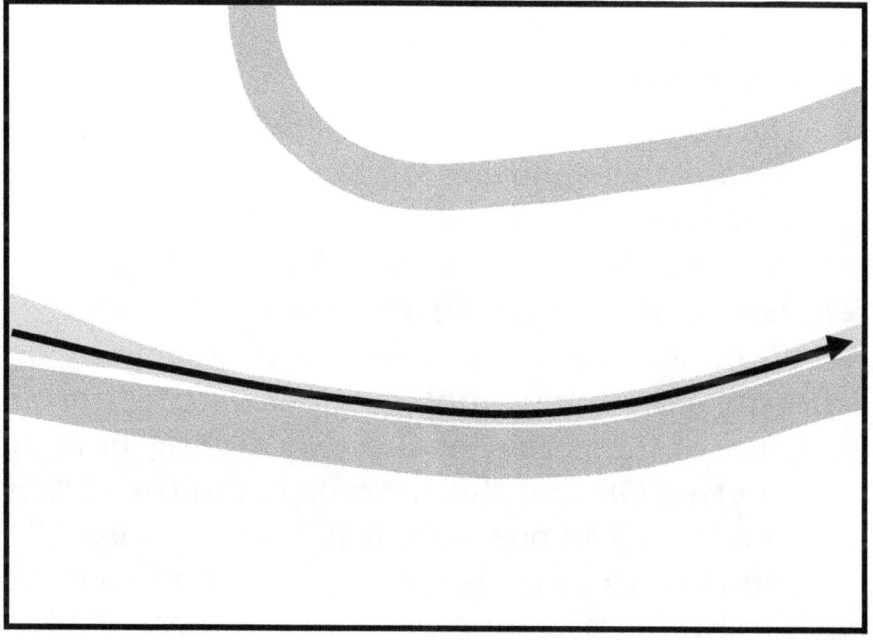

The first point of risk for cars intersecting is immediately following release by the starter, as the entering car must be careful not to wander to the right across the painted boundary lines on the uphill climb to Turn 1. On track cars will be coming at wide open throttle down the front straight and corner apexing Turn 1 adjacent to the outer of the two painted lines in excess of 120 mph, while the entering car is accelerating in second gear and not likely to be going more than 40 mph. The closure rate between two cars at this point can be in excess of 80 mph, with separation between the outer edge of the entry lane and the inside line of the main track demarked by only a few inches of space between the two painted lines. This corner apex point is down slope and beyond the crest of the hill, with visibility for both cars thus potentially affected.

The approaching on track car must mind its driving line to not intrude left beyond the right most of the two entry lane boundary lines, and the entering car should at all times keep well left of the left most of the two entry lane boundary lines.

While the starter should not be releasing an entering car when such a close encounter to potential intersection of the two driving lines of the entering car and the on track car at the corner apex of Turn 1 is possible, it is the responsibility of both drivers to be prepared for it and to drive safely with the presumption that it is a possibility.

The Merge

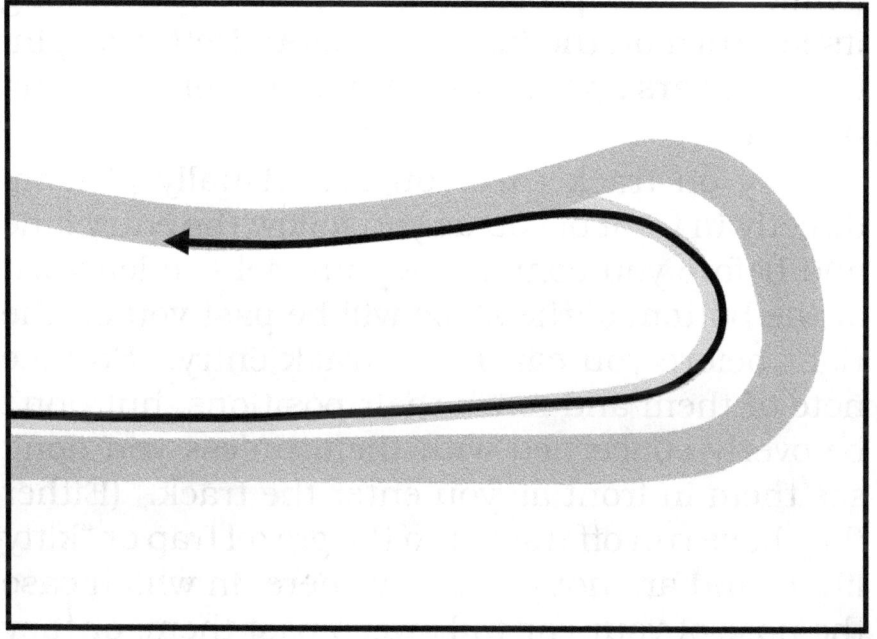

The second point of risk for cars intersecting is following entry to the track on approach to Turn 3. Cars exiting Turn 2 on track out will be at WOT from the right edge and immediately transitioning cross track to the left edge to prepare for entry to the left to right Turn 3. The speed of on track cars at the point of merger or blending of the driving line of the entry lane will in almost all cases be faster than the speed of the entering car. The entering car should use mirrors and listen for engine noise (the roar of an approaching car coming down the slope and unmistakable sound of making two or even three quick down shifts should make picking up the approach of any car straightforward, (even with helmet and ear protection) just prior to initiating its left turn on the inside of the Andretti Hairpin, to locate cars approaching from the right side and behind.

Any on track cars you can visually pick up directly in front of you as you follow the entry lane and before you commence your right to left turn at the bottom of the slope will be past you on the right before you can make track entry. So take note of them and mark their positions, but don't be overly concerned with them unless you don't see them in front as you enter the track. (Either they have run off track into the gravel trap or "kitty litter" and are not going anywhere, in which case the nose of your car will sweep past them, or they are slowed by being out of or on the ragged edge of control, in which case they could be anywhere and you need to be alert to the possibility they are not where they should be, and thus uncomfortably close to you, mandating potential evasive action on your part.)

As the nose of your car traverses the inside of Turn 2 faster than any on track car can drive through it, even with your head and direct vision swiveled to the left to mark your entry line, you should be able to note such an on track distress with your peripheral vision to the right side, and perhaps the tire squeal associated with a driver's fight for control, giving you time to decide what to do and time to do it.

It is the cars coming down the hill behind you that are usually of primary risk interest to you.

Note the corner worker station in the tower above and to your left as you descend the entry lane towards Turn 2. As you approach and enter the track surface quickly look over your right shoulder, stay left and accelerate quickly along the left edge of the track surface, and check your mirrors for any cars coming through the corner apex and accelerating out of Turn 2.

The entering car must not wander right of the driving line as the entry lane merges, but remain predictably and tightly along the left edge of the track surface.

Many entering cars will accelerate to speed that is sufficient to take Turn 3 at the limits of adhesion of their tires, and powerful cars will possibly even need to lift throttle or brake slightly before corner entry. An on track car abreast of you to the right on track entry will usually have greater speed than the entering car can muster, and will pass on the right side of the entering car, then transition from right to left in front of the entering car to the left edge of the surface to position itself on the driving line for the braking segment and corner entry.

The entering car will be at full throttle and may be very close to the passing car then drifting in front from right to left, and needs to watch for the inception of the on track passing car's braking segment before turn in to Turn 3, as the entering car may still be accelerating when the passing car initiates braking, with relative velocities then changing rapidly just before turn in.

The higher speed of the on track passing car will often require that its braking inception point occur earlier than the slower yet still accelerating car that is entering the track.

This will cause an "accordion" like closure of distance between the two cars in a short distance and space of time. Both drivers should be mindful and factor this in to their corner approach so that neither will be surprised, and avoid either a run up of the leading car's tailpipe by the entering car, or an over reaction by the entering car with an unbalancing brake input that is more than needed to keep a safe distance.

(**Beginner's note**: The entry lane is narrow, with a concrete wall on the left, fast cars on the right, and a sharp hairpin corner at the bottom of the hill on a ribbon of asphalt barely one car wide before track entry. That section cannot be negotiated at much more than 25 to 30 mph anyway, so take it easy. The fast driving is for the track, not the entry lane.

Stay well left of the lane separation lines going up hill and watch your right mirror for cars coming over the crest of the hill and through Turn 1 so you will be aware of their approach on the right from the exit of Turn 2.

As you enter the track the absolute speeds of both entering and on track cars are reasonably modest and the initial separations are usually the full width of the track. (I say "usually", but anything is possible on a race track, which is why you use your eyes, mirrors and ears to check anyway.)

If you are already on the track, then as you progress down the front straight you have time to scan the hot pit, starting grid area and entry lane to note whether any cars are being released that could become an issue at corner apex for Turn 1 or when you round Turn 2.

Remember, an entering car could be obscured by the bridge over the track at the start/finish line, or the entering driver moving more slowly than your expectation over the hill crest, or you may just fail to visually pick them up. So look again to the left after cresting Turn 1 and setting up your brake run into Turn 2.

The driver on track will be turning his/her head ninety degrees left as or shortly after the braking run is commenced and will have a full view of the entry lane and all cars within it and inside the corner while he/she is picking up the Turn 2 corner exit apex visually.

There is both room and time for both drivers to safely merge their cars together into the driving line before the next corner at Turn 3, especially if you are not surprised by a car you did not expect. This is one reason why, if you prepare properly and pay attention, a "hot track" entry to Laguna Seca is among the safer and better designed configurations to manage.)

Entry merge. *Stay along left edge of track surface during transition from entry lane to race track.*

Turn 1

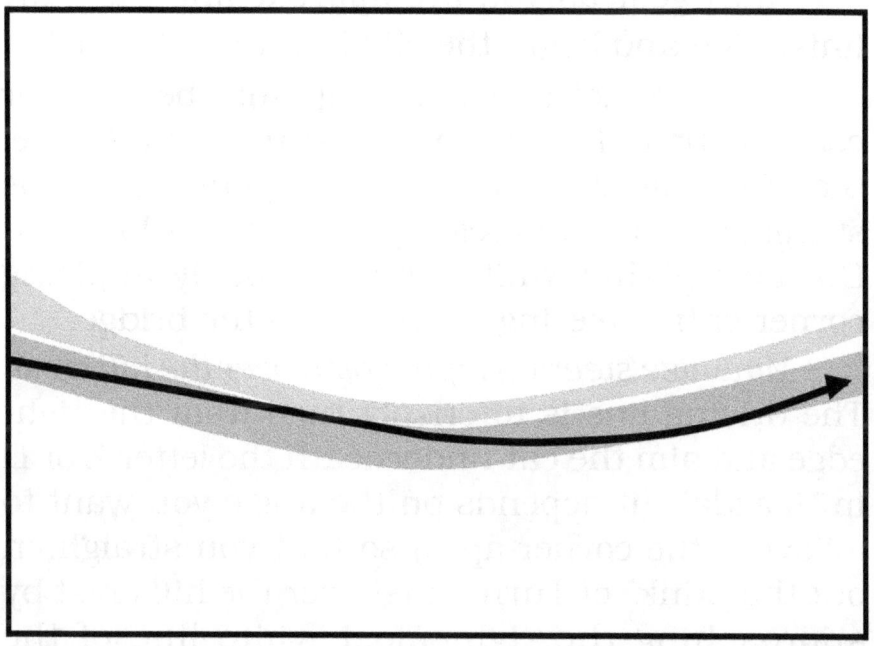

As you start the front straight at Laguna Seca following track out from Turn 11 you will be at the right edge of the track surface. The "straight" actually has a slight curvature of about 15 degrees from right to left at the pedestrian bridge over the start finish line, and again just past the crest of the hill of about 20 degrees at Turn 1, so stay along the right edge of the track surface as you exit Turn 11, up shift from either second or third gear depending on your selection going into Turn 11, quick check your gauges and mirrors as you accelerate up the straight, scan for cars being released for track entry by the starter from the hot pit, hold to the driving line and let faster drivers by on the left side, or similarly pass slower drivers on their left, grab fourth gear and then in some cars fifth gear as you are approaching the start finish line and begin the climb towards Turn 1.

If you cannot make your up shift before your corner entry to Turn 1 as you pass under the bridge, then up shift after turn in, when your steering is straightened out, and before you go over the hill crest. Do not up shift while simultaneously applying corner entry steering approaching the bridge.

Minimize steering input going over the hill crest. The driving line is to crisply turn from the right edge and aim the car underneath the letter Z or D in "Mazda", (it depends on the angle you want to follow at the corner apex) so that you straighten out the "kink" of Turn 1 just over the hill crest by approaching the right most white line of the painted double lines that separate the track entry lane on the left edge of the track from the track itself. If there is another car in the entry lane, adjust the driving line to keep extra safety separation distance between you.

Do not assume that even though the rule for the day is that cars must not enter the track surface at the top of Turn 1 that the entering car you have lost sight of, due to the bridge blocking your view, has not in fact done so.

Anything involving human judgment means that errors will occur, so drive prepared for the possibility of it happening.

(**Beginner's note**: The on track car must not intrude past or even crowd the white line or it will be into, or too close to, the entry lane area and at risk of clipping an entering car at a fast closure rate. *Keep your head and eyes up as you come down the straight* and view the entry lane to determine whether there are any cars being released for entry that may be at the Turn 1 corner apex by the time you arrive there, and simultaneously note the flag station at the start/finish line for any warning of trouble on the track through Turn 1 down to the entry to Turn 2 since you are approaching a hill crest and thus are blind to an upcoming segment of the track while going WOT in high gear).

There is a temptation to lift throttle as you crest the hill at WOT because you are blind to the down slope beyond... **don't do that**, any more than you should lean into a left hook in a boxing match. The inertial momentum when cresting the hill is going to remove weight and thus tire adhesion from the rear. In addition to further lightening the back end at more than 120 mph at precisely the moment you need it to be planted, and compounding the chance of a loss of grip and thus a left to right slide in the rear ("lift throttle over steer"), throttle lift will slow you down.

Align your driving line to the left to meet the corner apex, then stay with the throttle down to the floor straight (not curving with steering input) over the top of the hill. Note as you crest the hilltop that you are pointing towards the right edge, but at a point a lot farther down the track and sloping hill than you might have expected. *Don't immediately feed right to left steering input as you see the edge of the track.* Wait just a few fractions of a second more until you feel the back end of the car settle and regain grip beyond the hill crest, then gently put right to left steering into the wheel.

A tiny bit of steering input is all it usually takes. Rather than fight it, allow the lateral left to right inertia to ease the car towards the right edge of the pavement. As the steering input takes and the tires grab the surface, still with the throttle down (for experienced drivers to the floor), gently and smoothly unwind the steering and run along the right edge of the track surface. If the car is not gripping enough to turn or "under steering" because it is "pushing" through the steering input, you still have some track surface room when on the proper driving line to gently ease throttle a bit, possibly even unwind steering straight for just a moment as well, to let the front tires regain grip and then once more take the steering input from right to left, and gently squeeze back to WOT.

At this point the combination of the down hill slope with WOT in high gear, after chugging up the hill under the bridge, delivers an almost surprising rush of acceleration. With head and eyes up, you are looking directly into an approaching hairpin corner, probably as you are slammed by acceleration back into your seat. Don't be alarmed and lift your right foot, but stay on throttle until you reach your predetermined braking inception point. Follow the right edge sharply downhill until you are almost, but not quite, at your initial braking segment for entry to Turn 2, the Andretti Hairpin. Note the corner worker in the tower to the left for any warnings before you begin your braking segment. You should have checked your mirrors in the front straight and know where everyone behind you was and should be now, but a quick check again now is worthwhile.

(**Beginner's note**: Until you have an understanding of how your car responds to Turn 1, it is advisable to lift throttle before the crest of the hill just a touch to let the wind resistance, uphill slope and gravity slow the car, then squeeze back on throttle, not necessarily all the way, to sit the rear of the car down, again all **before** the crest of the hill. When you lift throttle the air resistance pushes the front of the car down and weight transfers forward from the rear and thus "lightens" or "loosens" the rear, so do it with the steering as straight as possible.

Gradually work your way up to going WOT over the hill crest so that you do not lose control of the car with a panic lift at the top your first couple of times around the track! The down slope acceleration can be alarming, especially as your nose is pointed directly at a hairpin turn that continues to descend, and your speed will be well beyond any experience you should have had as a street driver. It takes time to become accustomed to speeds beyond twice the legal limit on highways. And it takes time to learn the thresh hold braking capability of your car at high speed and down hill. Work your way up to learning those limits in gradual stages and small increments (perhaps two or three feet at most... certainly not ten!), picking out a braking reference on the track each time for consistency.

Avoid visual fixation on the turn, and keep your chin and eyes up, not driving "off the nose" of the car with a focus point only twenty or thirty feet in front, a common habit when you are used to driving in city traffic at twenty miles per hour. In addition, where an advanced driver may have the wheels of their car aligned precisely along the edge of the track surface or a couple of inches from it, a beginner should leave a safe margin of two or even three feet all around the track. Give yourself some more room to work with. As your abilities improve, you can gradually reduce the margins, and be adjusting your reference points in terms of inches).

No matter what your experience level, always stay safely within your limits as a driver, the limits of the car you are driving, and the condition of the track.

Entry to Turn 1, approaching hill crest. Note car in entry lane to left and double white lines. Keep to right of right most white line.

Turn 1. Note apex is after hill crest and down slope.

Turn 2 apex. *Vision should be far left on track out point.*

Turn 2 track out. *Vision should be on transition to left edge of track. Check mirrors. Note entering car ahead.*

Turn 2

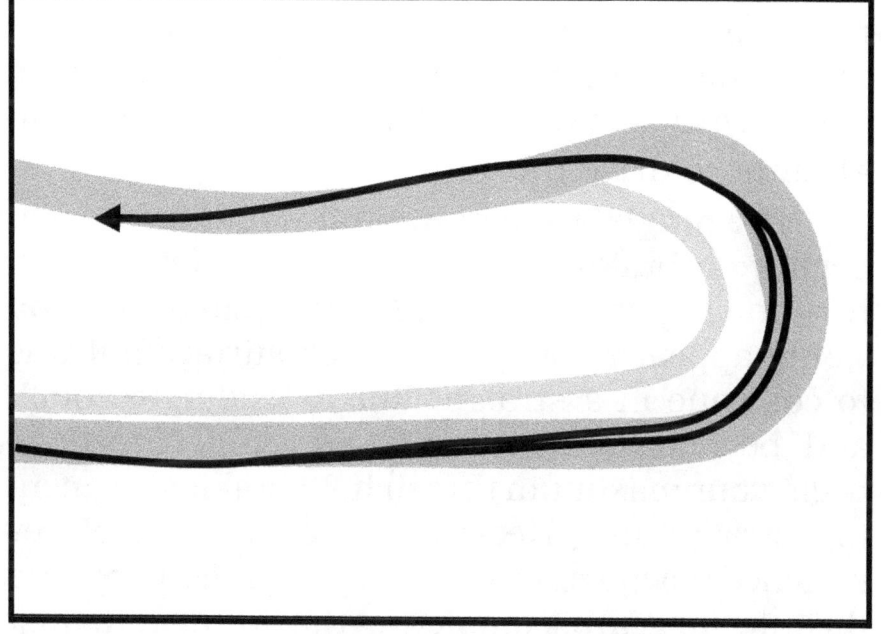

The Andretti hairpin is shaped like a "fish hook", bending almost 210 degrees from right to left, and then opening back to the right with a slight bend of about 10 degrees. There are several ways to take this turn, among them the "double apex" and the classic very late "single apex". Which approach you choose is a function of your personal driving comfort and skills, car capabilities, and driving strategy. *You should try to become comfortable with both techniques.*

If you have not driven the course before, it is highly advisable to ride with an instructor behind the wheel and have both approaches demonstrated to you. Pay attention, then pull into the pits, ask questions, get answers, and then switch seats and have the instructor ride as passenger with you driving to help with your technique, and give you comments in a download when your session is completed, before you attempt to drive the course solo.

The single apex approach. Just before you begin your braking run, and while still on throttle, turn in crisply from the right edge such that you would appear to bisect the track surface if it was to continue in a straight line extending through and beyond the turn, and then get off throttle to begin your maximum thresh hold braking segment in a straight line. Heel/toe two or three quick rev matched down shifts, or one if you prefer to bypass the interim gears, completing the down shifts just before finishing the straight braking segment and commencing turn in.

While under straight braking and down shifting, turn your head and mark the apex of the turn almost 90 degrees to your left side and off your shoulder as you begin turn in. This is critical to taking the corner fast, and in visually picking up any cars in the entry lane that might be a factor as you

TURN 2   41

approach Turn 3 after corner exit from Turn 2. There is nothing magical about looking out the side window opening (the windows will be down) of the car rather than through the windshield while braking and down shifting. In either instance you are not looking at the shift lever, steering wheel or pedals!

Using your peripheral vision to the right to pick your turn in point, ease pressure smoothly off your brake pedal as you begin your turn in and trail off the pressure ("trail braking") still with your eyes on the corner apex, so that you can rotate the rear of the car from left to right. As the rear end gets "loose" and slides, use counter steer and as the rear tires regain grip, squeeze gently back on throttle to align the yaw or rotation towards the corner apex, and shift weight back to the rear of the car to further increase rear grip. As the nose begins to point towards the apex, also begin to unwind the steering and continue to roll on the power as the back end settles down and grabs the pavement. There is a slight bit of favorable camber out to the mid track line. The corner continues to slope down hill all the way from corner entry to corner exit, which further promotes rotation/slide.

Don't get too greedy with the power, or you will transfer from a weight forward over steer induced by trail braking and the lateral inertia in the down slope turn, to a "throttle on" (or too much power to the drive wheels) over steer and spin out, or even a loss of grip to the front wheels (remember you have transferred weight from front to rear with the application of more throttle which reduces front wheel grip) and a "push" or under steer, so you need to control the car between these two extremes. There is a decent band of power choice available between the two extremes that mark loss of adhesion, so think more of a "maintenance" throttle level that does not transfer too much weight either forward or rearward.

Avoid the "porpoise" effect of unbalancing your weight between the front and the rear, and keep the car as level from front to rear as you can through the transition. Try not to drift beyond mid track line, as that will be too deep and long a route and on a "high" driving line that is up in the adhesion loosening rubber marbles and grit. As you get to the corner apex point, which is along the blue and white painted rumble stripes and at the raised concrete curb just inside them, you should have the throttle on or close to the floor and the steering almost completely unwound. Once again the lateral inertia from coming through the corner will push the car towards the right edge of the track as you accelerate out of the corner.

(Beginner's note: Do **not** trail the brake on this turn. *Finish your braking in a straight line, then breathe on a touch of throttle to sit the rear of the car down gently,* transitioning weight from front to rear for more even balance, and maintain it. As you come around the turn gradually roll on power as you come to and through the corner apex, and with additional lap experience gradually work up your speed through the corner.

Work up your corner entry speed and depth of corner entry point in small stages. If the car does not respond to steering input you are exceeding the grip of the front tires, or under steering, and will need to ease off throttle, and possibly straighten steering a touch, to regain grip for the front tires, and then return to putting in steering and more throttle. The surface is very wide and there is good room for recovery from under steer unless you have entered the corner at excessive speed, in which case you will push until you leave the track and enter the expansive gravel "kitty litter" trap, which will grab and hold you. You will likely sit there buried to your axle hubs until the tow truck comes to collect you with the entire session black flagged, engendering less than charitable sentiments towards your ruination of the session for everyone else in the run group.

So, take it easy with Turn 2, and *concentrate on flowing smoothly through the corner, working on your head rotation and vision, downshifting, turn in and corner exit acceleration techniques while hitting your apex point cleanly.* You can't go fast through there unless you are doing all of those correctly anyway!)

The double apex approach. You will need to pick an "entry" as well as an "exit" apex for the corner. The entry apex is of course on the left inside edge of the track, and you will approach it slightly differently than the single apex approach. Coming down the right edge of the track you will make a sharper angled turn in from the right than the single apex approach, because the geometry of the driving line takes you to the inside edge on corner entry, which is not the case for the single exit apex approach.

You want to put your left front wheel across the top of your apex point. Finish your braking and down shifts by the time you reach your entry apex, (unless you want to promote some rotation with a bit of trail braking, in which case you will still have some brake pedal engagement at the entry apex), get your head up and swiveled over to mark your exit apex point, be feeding in your right to left steering, gradually applying throttle to hook up the rear tires and accelerate through the exit apex.

The path followed by the car in this approach is shorter in distance through the corner than the single apex approach, and thus potentially with that shorter distance would allow a car to reach the exit apex in less time... but also with a sharper, smaller and potentially somewhat slower radius arc to the corner than the single apex approach, which would potentially increase the time to cover the same distance... so you will have to experiment to see which approach works best for you and your car.

As soon as you have marked the nose of the car on the corner apex at Turn 2, irrespective of whether you have used the single or double apex approach... stop looking at it. The car is going to go there. You should have your eyes up, quickly marking the corner exit track out point at the edge on the right (Remember the "fishhook" bend as the right edge will come to you a bit quicker than you might be expecting), and then looking beyond to the cross track position on the left edge to begin your entry to Turn 3.

Scan visually to the left for any cars that may be entering the track from the entry lane, and decide whether you will a) pass them on their right with time and distance satisfactory for you to get settled safely on the far left edge of the track in front of them, or you will b) slip in behind them to follow the entering car through Turn 3. Be careful about diving into the corner to the "inside" of the driving line on the right against any car on Turn 3, as there is a good chance you will have to slow down to avoid running off the left edge of the track on corner exit track out. With the shorter radius driving arc you have now forced on yourself by cutting inside the optimal driving line, your overall time going through the corner would have been much better had you used patience and discretion to slip behind and follow the entering car... which car is going to have so much better corner exit speed out of Turn 3 than you will have that they will probably pass you before Turn 4 anyway. "Slower" can become "faster" sometimes.

(Beginner's note: Throughout your runs at any track, *work on your vision "downfield"* so that *you are never just looking off the nose of the car, but ahead to the next one or even two marks for your drive. As you approach corners these will typically be, in order, your braking point, turn in point, corner apex, track out point, and driving line to the next corner. Gather in the braking and turn in points in a smooth motion of your head and then use peripheral vision to initiate your inputs as you look ahead to the corner apex and track out points. Never allow yourself to be surprised and thus forced to use "reactive" inputs because your field of vision was focused too close to the car.)*

Turn 3. *Note lateral load transfer on outside tires of lead car in mid corner.*

Turn 3

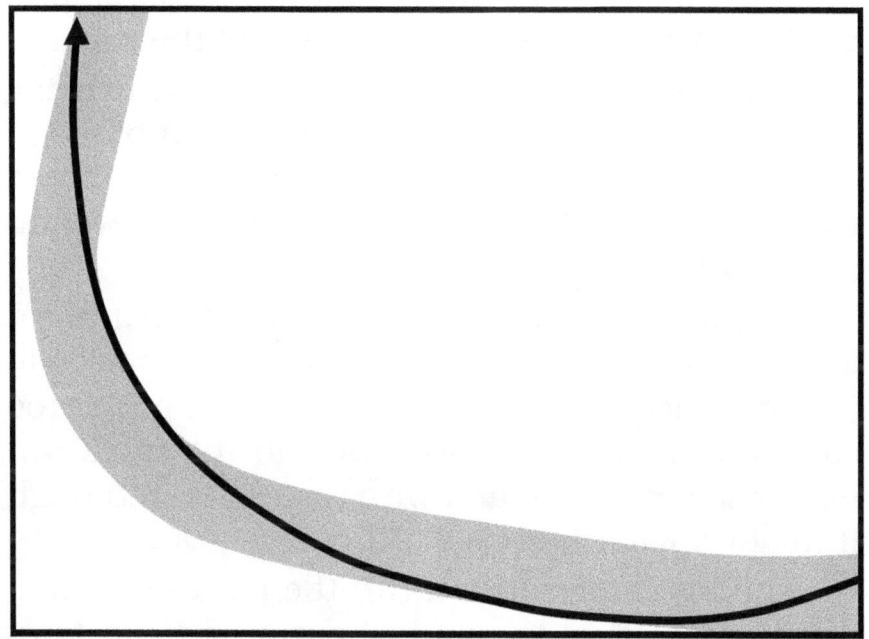

Smoothly turn from the right track edge on exit from Turn 2 towards the left of the #3 brake marker on the left edge of the track, note the corner worker station ahead, up shift, stay on power, be vigilant for entering cars along the track entry blend line, gently turn slightly right to slip along the left edge of the track, and firmly brake between the #2 and #1 brake markers in a straight line to set your corner entry speed.

A late apex, late turn in is important on this approximately 90 degree corner as it is a diminishing radius with a flat to slightly off camber surface at corner exit. Early corner entry can put you off the edge of the track surface to the left, or even spinning, at corner exit. Your corner apex is late, in the last half to one third of the blue and white rumble stripes on the inside of the turn.

For safety, gradually work your way up to being WOT coming out of this corner, as the combination of speed and tightened turning radius can exceed the grip of your tires surprisingly quickly, even in a car with modest torque.

(**Beginners note**: This is a corner that grabs a lot of cars and drivers, especially at the novice to low intermediate skill level, who get on power too early and run out of pavement during track out for corner exit, so treat it with respect even though it might appear benign.

The instinctive lift off throttle for a beginning driver who is concerned about going too fast, transitions weight forward while the car is turning to the right, lightening the rear and promoting a right to left spin of the back end of the car.

This is a corner where novice drivers are frequently two or three feet from the proper corner apex, and follow an inconsistent driving line from lap to lap. Pick a precise apex point along the driving line that is the size of a coin, and try to hit that point with your right front tire every lap. To do it consistently you will quickly discover that *the corner entry point becomes the key.*

Following track out to the left edge, stay along the left edge of the track at full throttle, and up shift before reaching the braking zone for entry to Turn 4.)

Turn 3 track out. *Once settled, pick your corner turn in point, check mirrors, gauges, and corner worker station.*

Turn 4 apex. *Vision focus is towards track out point at far end of grand stands on left.*

Turn 4 track out. *Note striped section on right edge of track as transition mark for your driving line.*

Turn 4

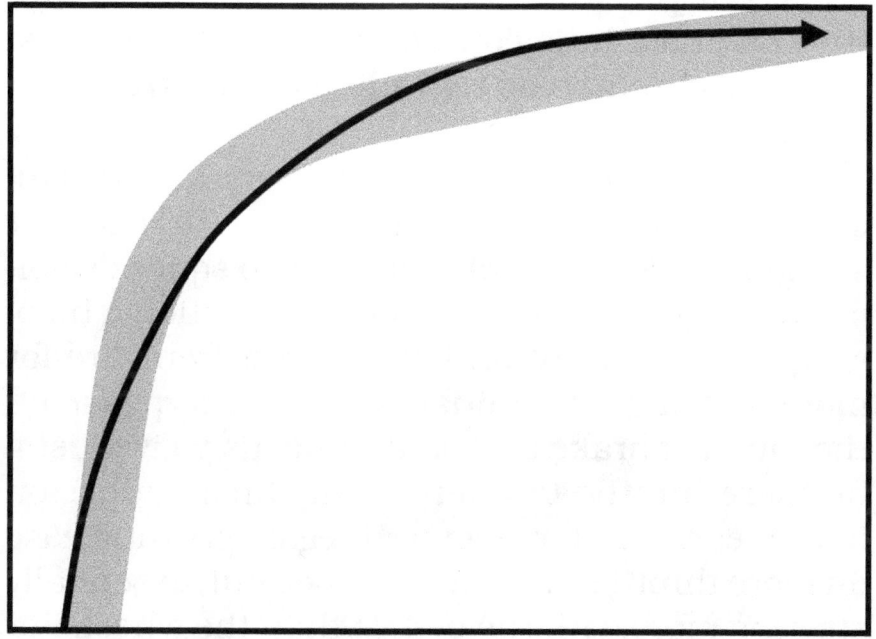

A moderately powered and well handling car may take Turn 4 without lifting throttle, but many more powerful cars may have more grip demand on their tires under WOT than the tires have grip to give. For those cars it may be necessary to breathe off the throttle, or even add a light touch of brake before or even during the first few feet of entry to Turn 4 to help set a bit more weight over the front tires to add grip at the corner entry turn in point.

You can trail the brake slightly to induce a little over steer, allowing you to point the nose a few degrees to the right and thus unwind steering a bit earlier, and get back on throttle a bit earlier and harder, indeed to use relatively little steering at all, but you want to settle the back down with throttle and a little counter steer as this is a fast turn with an increasing radius as you track out to exit.

Some of the more skilled drivers in powerful cars can use another approach, if the car suspension is amenable, which is to squeeze a bit on the brake with the left foot to transition a bit of weight on the front and set the left front tire for more steering bite, initiate corner entry, ease off the touch of brake and simultaneously give just a bit more throttle to intentionally break adhesion in the rear, counter steer and regain grip and ease on more throttle once straightened out, essentially steering more with the pedals than the wheel. For others with adequate front tire grip, a little bit of wheel flick with the hands and a quick counter steer catch can work as well.

This corner is pretty fast, so it is not recommended that you explore left foot braking or rotation technique for the first time here. Skid pads and car control courses are where you begin to learn and play with these and many other techniques, and then slower speed corners on track where you can first apply it. Any kind of over steer in high speed corners is to be avoided by all but the most advanced skill level drivers, as a high speed slide recovery is more difficult, and the consequences of failure more severe. The sideways slide into the gravel trap on the left of the track surface at a high speed means you have enough momentum to potentially roll the car when the tires dig in.

This is a corner that illustrates well how you should be using all of the track surface, from the corner apex on the right edge all the way to track out on the left edge. If you are not using all of the surface, then you need to adjust your corner entry point and speed through corner exit so that you do use all the track surface, while still maintaining adhesion. If you are going WOT all the way to and through corner entry of Turn 4, and still not generating enough momentum relative to your tire grip to push you to the left edge on corner exit track out, then you can begin to adjust the driving line to shorten the arc radius of the turn to shorten the distance traversed.

The flag station is directly ahead of you as you approach Turn 4, and as your vision to the right and through the corner is blocked on this, and indeed on many of the corners, make a habit of always noting the flag worker early in your approach for maximum warning time in case something beyond your field of vision has gone awry. Laguna Seca corner worker stations are well placed, typically elevated above the surface in small towers (other than at the Corkscrew), and highly visible to the on track driver.

At Turn 4 there is a wall on the left that you can hit if you go off track. With a long, level following straight you want power on as early as you can for maximum corner exit speed, but not at the risk of dropping your left wheels off the track surface. The corner exit is increasing radius, but the power application is earlier than many, and as you have now noted there can be a choice of approaches to corner entry, so for some cars the apex can be a touch early because they can hold to full power while turning and still retain grip, and for others the apex can be slightly beyond the middle of the turn, so be patient with this corner and learn how your car is reacting to it.

As you reach track out with the left side tires on the edge of the pavement you are looking ahead to the right and marking the striped section on the right edge of the track as your left to right transition mark.

There is a left to right kink of about 20 degrees in the geometry of the track here. If you swing the radius arc of your turn correctly you will finish your corner exit from Turn 4 smoothly aligned precisely straight along the right edge of the track after the kink and roaring towards Turn 5 at WOT.

CORNER EXIT TRANSITION FROM TURN 4

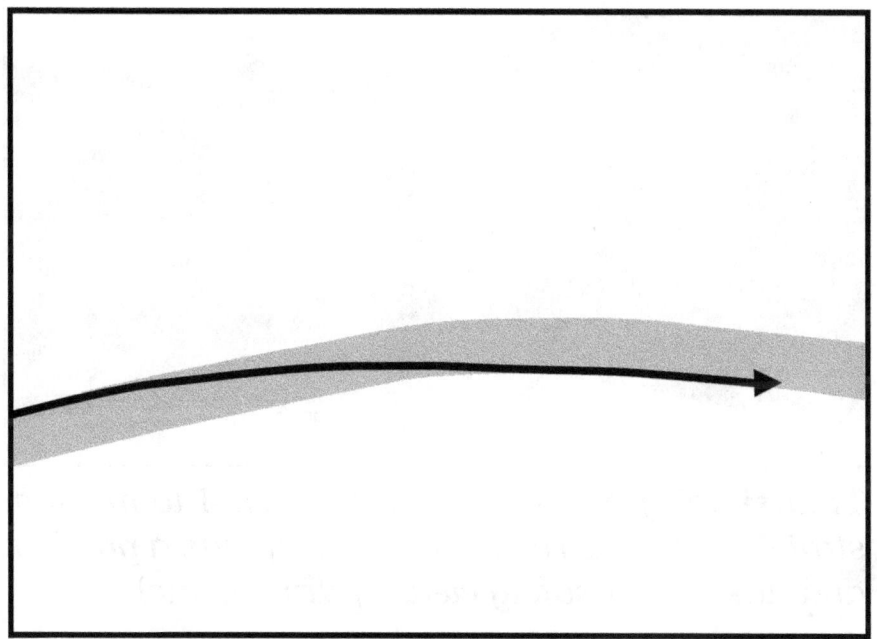

(**Beginners note**: Staying WOT at corner exit you straighten out the kink in the track surface on the right side and continue down the straight to Turn 5. Check your mirrors and while holding to the driving line let faster drivers by on the left. Check your gauges with a quick glance if it is safe to do so.

Concentrate on staying as far right as you safely can and pick out your braking point and turn in point in one glance. Look up and note the track out of Turn 5 to see that it is clear of any cars that might have spun or drifted off track edge, and check the flag station at the end of the straight before turn in.)

Transition *from corner exit at Turn 4 to medium straight entering Turn 5. (Car on left has a problem and has pulled safely clear of driving line)*

Turn 5. *Note positive camber slope of this corner. Vision should be focused left on the track out point beyond lead car.*

Turn 5

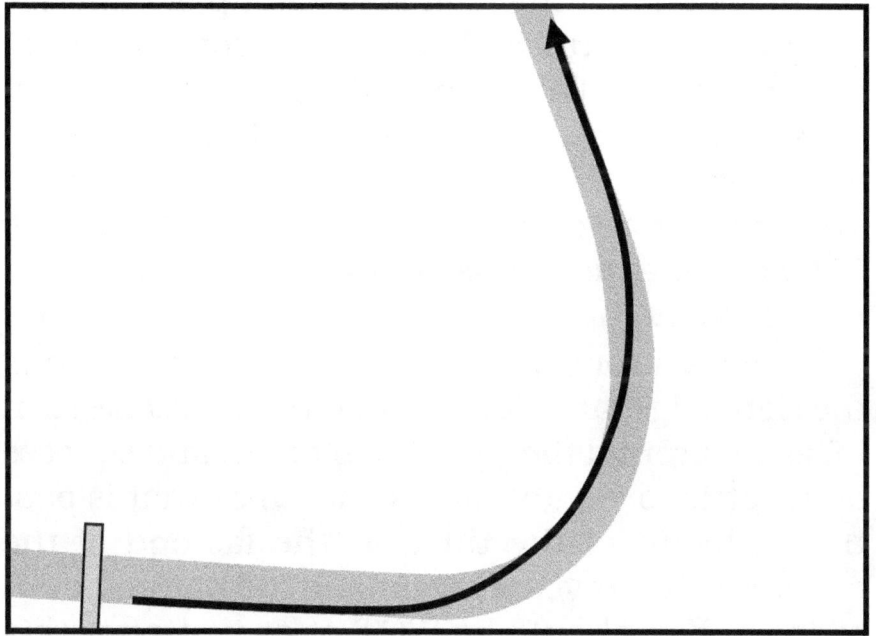

As you make the corner approach run down the straight, again check your mirrors, gauges, and note the corner worker station low and to the right at the end of the straight on the outside of the right to left corner. You will be approaching redline in your highest or next to highest gear when you begin your straight braking segment for this corner.

There is a great temptation to take this corner too early and too quickly, in part because it begins a steep uphill climb and one wants to maintain momentum, not lose speed as a result of over braking. This is just as applicable in a 600 bhp beast as in a 120 bhp "momentum" racer. Every car is a "momentum" car in this corner.

Turn 5 is absolutely critical to achieving fast lap times on this track. It sets you up not only for a hard uphill run to Turn 6, but for maximum speed through Turn 6 and then up the steepest climb on the course through the Rahal Straight and Turn 7. Thus, *maximizing exit speed out of Turn 5 to tackle a three hundred foot vertical climb is among the most critical driving skill challenges on the circuit.*

Make a strong straight thresh hold brake along the right edge, and downshift, effect a precise turn in, again around the #1 brake marker, and squeeze on throttle to yet another corner apex that is past the midpoint of the turn, at the far end of the concrete motorcycle curb inside the painted curb stripes. You should be WOT at or just after this corner apex, and the strong positive camber sloping from the outside right track edge, especially from the mid track point down to the inside left edge of the track, will help you maintain adhesion under full throttle through the corner. In fact, the positive camber permits you to apply more power or adjust your apex point earlier, but use some care as the positive camber flattens out as you drift towards the edge on the right. You therefore must be mindful to not unwind your steering too rapidly during track out.

(Beginners note: A lot of drivers enter this corner too early/fast, and as a result need to lift throttle or even brake slightly in the corner or even during track out as they are going uphill to avoid going two wheels off on the right edge. This wastes a huge amount of momentum that cannot be recovered up the long climb to Turn 8, and in some cases also causes the car to spin. So the mantra of "slow in-fast out" is very critical as well as being safer for this corner. Get your braking done before turn in and squeeze on power all the way through the corner, and you will be rewarded with a good pull up the hill, no matter what the power of your car.)

This is another good time to check your gauges quickly, if you did not have the chance to do so in the last straight, as you pull up the hill and before you get to the bridge. If you have a horsepower/weight ratio advantage over a car positioned just in front of you going into Turn 5, and you have executed the corner better with higher exit speed, you may be able to pass on the left side going up the hill. But be sure that you can safely get all the way back over to the right edge of the pavement before your braking segment and corner entry for Turn 6, or else wait for another opportunity.

Laguna Seca has a sound limit of 90 or 92 decibels for many outings, and the sound station is located to the right of the track out point following corner exit from Turn 5. A violation of the sound limit is usually reported to you by the corner worker station to the left of the track at Turn 7 on the Rahal Straight with the "meatball" flag (a black flag with an orange circle in the middle which denotes equipment problems on your car) requiring you to proceed to the starter for communication of your decibel reading, and retirement to the paddock to work changes on the car to lower the sound output before you will be allowed back on to the track.

Most groups only allow a car three violations of the sound rule, and on the third violation the car must be retired for the balance of the day. County fines of up to $1,000 per lap once one has passed the allowable number of offending laps are potentially applicable at the time of this writing, so it is best to get your noise management issues taken care of before you arrive so that you can enjoy your day at the track fully by riding in your car, not wrenching underneath it. Almost all stock engines with OEM exhaust systems will have no trouble passing this sound restriction. Track only cars with straight pipes or side dumps, and street legal cars with forced induction (superchargers/turbochargers) matched with after market high performance exhausts are more likely to encounter sound limit violations.

Your track day sponsor may be able to connect you with other enthusiasts that run a comparable set up to yours so that you can discuss sound management approaches that will keep you within the specified limits for your track day. These may include different and more restrictive exhaust systems, exhaust tip turn outs, lowering supercharger and turbocharger boost levels, etc.

Turn 5 track out. *Stay right, check mirrors and gauges. Corner entry to Turn 6 and corner worker tower are not visible to driver from this position.*

Exit *from Andretti Hairpin with double pass developing to left side after "point by" signal from lead car.*

Prepare for the Unexpected

A few words about safely getting by a suddenly distressed car in front of you. This section of track at Laguna Seca presents a good spot to remind ourselves that all of us are out on a track to have a good time as safely as possible. But sometimes events will unfold that are not on the menu of "good time", and you need to be prepared to deal with them.

Most of the occasions on track when a car gets into difficulty that presents a potential or actual risk to others, the corner workers at their flag stations and connected by their radio headsets to each other will be signaling track conditions in front of you that allow you to take appropriate and safe measures well in advance to manage the hazard. Know the flags!

Most events involving an off track excursion or other hazard transpire from start to finish in a matter of only a few seconds, and somewhere on the track other than right in front of you. With typical track lengths of 2.5 to 3.5 miles, average lap speeds of 70 to 80 mph and lap times of between 1:45 and 3:00 minutes, you often have an abundance of time and space to be warned and prepared. By the time you arrive at the scene, the car involved may already be back on track and on its way such that you never even see it before it reaches the track exit. Or the last wisps of dust and tire smoke are wafting away and the car is stationary.

But eventually, and it could be your first day out on the track or your fiftieth, somebody is going to "lose it" in front of you in close enough proximity that advance corner worker flag signals are not relevant.

You are on your own judgment and skill to avoid disaster, and it is on you immediately.

It could be a loss of control by the driver of that car. It could be the surprise of a part falling off such as a lug nut, exhaust pipe, body panel, even a drive shaft, or a fluid being discharged from a blown coolant hose or engine oil. It could be a small animal bolting across the track, or a plastic bag blowing on to your windshield. It could be you losing your brakes, or having other control problems. Your engine may quit, clutch pedal stick to the floor, or steering fail. All things mechanical can break, and many of them do break.

I recall a car losing control at an HPDE at Laguna Seca because it ran over a very large fresh water crawfish that made a dash across the track in a high speed corner, and the car lost traction and spun. Nobody was hurt, the car was not damaged and there were plenty of jokes and laughter later at the driver download session about langostino for dinner, whether anyone had a spatula in their tool boxes and should the corner worker have seen the crustacean and waved the track surface obstacle flag (or should a new "lobster" flag be immediately added to the inventory of flags for the track), but it certainly was no fun for that driver when he lost traction as a result of squishing the hapless trespasser.

Desert tortoises are known to have crossed the track at Spring Mountain in Pahrump, Nevada, (where there are strict rules to do everything safely to avoid the precious creatures) and deer, dogs, possum, raccoon, coyote, squirrel, jack rabbit and other creatures are not uncommon jaywalkers on many circuits elsewhere. Wet leaves, pine needles, dust, dirt, sand and grit, rubber marbles, not to mention oil, water, coolant, brake fluid, steering fluid... the possibilities of surprise challenge are without limit. You don't get to choose, you must be ready for anything. Every lap is new and different and you must be focused in your concentration without lapses.

If you are following another car, even at a distance of 20 or 30 car lengths, you should have them in your vision clearly as your head should be up. This section of Turns 3 through 5 reflect a classic series of corners where you are vision impaired much beyond the corner apex, so you need to be watchful of the corner worker coming to the apex of the turn, and be monitoring the car in front and aware of whether it has negotiated the track out on the right or left edge successfully. If that car in front has dropped one or more wheels off the edge, you have time to back off the throttle and give room and time for the events in front of you to unfold, including if necessary to slow down or stop or even deliberately leave the track surface should that be the safest alternative left available to you.

You should not assume that because the car in front of you has drifted off track surface to the side that it is safe to pass on the other side or that the other driver is even aware of your presence. Indeed it should be presumed that the driver ahead has his/her hands very full with the challenge of car control and has lost all focus on everything else.

One risk is that they could compound their track out error of running off the edge with an overcorrection that launches them across the track from the opposite side, hammering the throttle and taking a path that could simply cause one of you to go nose first into the side of the other in a violent collision.

As the overtaking car it is your responsibility to manage a pass safely.

You have the advantage of being in control of your car and seeing everything in front of you, while the car in front of you does not. Accordingly, with your priority being safety, and not the achievement of your personal best lap time on this lap, slow down. This does not mean that you should slam on your brakes and create a second potential hazard to cars approaching from behind, and a compounding of the danger and complexity of safe passage. Rather, with the knowledge of who is behind you and how close from having checked your mirrors on approach to the corner, you begin your safe evasion of the problem in front.

If the driver in front exhibits a controlled exit and slowing off track, safely pull off line to the center or even farther away and pass, then merge back on line to the edge and set up for the next corner.

If the driver in front is spinning on the track surface, apply brake smoothly and slow down while carefully watching the direction of his momentum and what the car is doing. If he/she is "both feet in" (brake and clutch pedals fully depressed) and sliding to the edge to a stop, stay oriented to the opposite edge and manage your speed to be able to take safe evasive action if there is a sudden and unexpected change in the direction or dynamic of the car in front, such as a roll or flip or sudden regaining of traction so that you can evade or stop without colliding.

You want to get safely by the event if you can, so that approaching cars from behind are not an additional danger to you or the car in trouble. Once you are past the event and out of immediate danger yourself, you can follow the directions of the corner workers, which may be nothing as the track in front of you is clear, or a simple yellow flag caution, or a black flag to all drivers to come in to the pits under caution, or even a red flag to all drivers to come to a full and complete on course stop until directed to restart.

What a lot of your study to driving a course efficiently does is highlight the places where you might get into trouble, which conveniently is where other drivers are likely to get into trouble, and how and why. You analyze what you ought to do as a driver should that trouble occur to you, so that you have prepared for it and can react quickly... there is no time for leisurely reflection in the midst of the challenge. You should know where the safer run off areas are, and where the walls or other obstacles to avoid are. You should have already determined what you need to be doing and why and how before you ever get there. You should also have maintained sufficient track awareness that you know whether there are cars approaching from behind so that your recovery efforts are going to be among the safer options.

That preparation for what you are going to do if you get in trouble also helps you to understand what the likely dynamics of a car in front of you are going to be should it be in distress, and what is likely to transpire as the driver struggles for control, so you can act accordingly as the following car to avoid further mishap to either of you.

This should be a part of your preparation and study for driving every corner on every course before you strap in to your car to drive it. And then closely note in your orientation laps with your instructors, and in your own warm up laps, the action options and whether they match up to your expectations from your track map reviews, in car videos you have watched, and discussions with other drivers. If the sponsor organization offers an orientation ride around the track for drivers, by all means do it. Even better, try to get the opportunity to walk or bicycle around the track.

A slow, close up look at the track will reveal subtle undulations, changes in camber, surface grip conditions, run off area characteristics and much more. If you can do it with four or five other drivers, you will pick up much valuable information during your conversation as you journey around the circuit.

Turn 6 apex. *Note nose down "dip" in corner.*

Turn 6 exit. *Note center track position of leading cars. Rahal straight will bend back from left side to meet them from that driving line.*

Turn 6

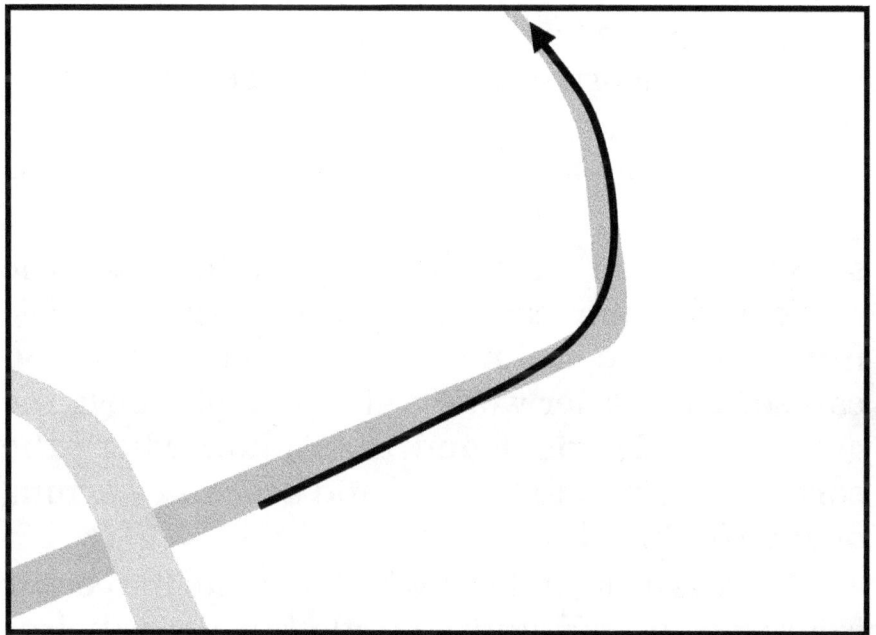

Up shift after Turn 5 as you reach your shift point rpm, usually just before midway up the hill by the sound station on the right. As you come to the bridge the steep incline decreases to a short plateau and the car begins to accelerate more briskly.

The transition from this plateau into Turn 6 really depends on the speed and handling characteristics of your car. A lower power car may be able to proceed through the corner at WOT without lifting. A higher power car may need to briefly make a short foot drag on the brakes, and then reapply the throttle as turn in to the corner is initiated. Do not wait too long to initiate this braking section as Turn 6 is a deceptively difficult corner that can be taken very fast, but is punitive if you do it incorrectly. The car will get unsettled if the driver is indecisive or incorrect in approach.

Watch the right edge of the track and before you reach the bridge the elevated corner worker station on the right should come into view. The track surface and cars in the corner are not visible from this angle and below the hill crest, but you can see the corner worker station high above the ground on the right and thus know where the corner is located to the left, and get early warning of any troubles there.

There is a slight downward bank into the corner from right to left, and a subtle but nevertheless significant dip at the apex point in the middle of the corner. You must be on throttle going through the dip to keep the rear of the car planted or the compression and release of the rear springs combined with the right to left inertia from the turn may lighten the rear, induce a left to right spin and leave you pointing at the wall on the inside of the corner. This is especially true if you lift throttle as the rear is lightening and the car turning. When the wheels regain traction during a left to right rotational slide, the car may then be launched directly at the wall on the inside of the corner. The many colorful paint splashes along the wall are testament to the frequency with which it happens.

One technique to work your way up to speed in this corner is to be a bit slower at entry than you think you should be, and after turn in "straighten out" with a touch of left to right steering at the mid corner section through the dip at the corner apex as you roll on the power and hold it down through the apex. Then, once you are clear of the dip and the rear end has recompressed and stabilized, add a little right to left steering input if you need to. Unless you have huge power and speed through this segment the incline that begins just after this corner apex, combined with the wide track out space to the right edge, should allow you plenty of room to remain on the track surface at WOT. Use all of the track surface for track out and resist the temptation to hold on steering lock to get across the track to the left edge too quickly. Keep increasing your speed through the entry to apex of Turn 6 in gradual increments until the inertia is taking you to the far right edge stripes.

(**Beginners note**: Down shift one gear on the straight brake section before the turn in, as this will help you to stay on throttle and accelerate more briskly out of the corner. The advanced driver who can maintain higher momentum through the corner will not have to down shift. However this downshift will allow you to negotiate this corner with less risk of losing control while you work on your technique. Once you have developed a smooth transition through the corner and have felt the compression and release of the rear springs going through the dip, and taken note of how your car behaves, you can cautiously try going through the corner without a down shift and without throttle lift. It will still be wise to not be WOT in the higher gear until you have gathered a lot of experience in car control and have a lot of experience with the corner.)

While Turn 3 will gather up and spin novice drivers aplenty, with relatively modest consequences from a slow speed corner, Turn 6 is dangerous to the intermediate and high intermediate level drivers who are going quite a bit faster, but have not yet developed the car control skills or thorough understanding of how this corner can in a split fraction of a second throw the car's rear end around as the driver determines he is going too fast and makes a momentary reactive lift of throttle.

If you discover that you are going too fast to negotiate the corner, do not lift throttle or put more steering in (both of which can promote a loss of control and an encounter with the inside wall), but instead straighten out the steering, get through the dip, add some straight line braking after the dip, and recover with reduced speed to then steer and keep the car on the surface at the right edge. If that is still not manageable, just slow as much as you can and go in a straight line off the track into the wide kitty litter trap on the right. That might be embarrassing, but it is safer than a wild spin and possible encounter with the wall on the left.

This corner highlights how you can improve your chances of making it through a corner by understanding where and how you are likely to encounter difficulty, and what you can do to recover control with the least risk of injury to yourself or damage to your car.

Rahal Straight. Line up approach angle for entry to Turn 8 from left edge of track.

Exit from Turn 7 and transition towards entry to Turn 8. Note crest of hill as entry to corner bends to the right.

Turn 7 - the "Rahal Straight"

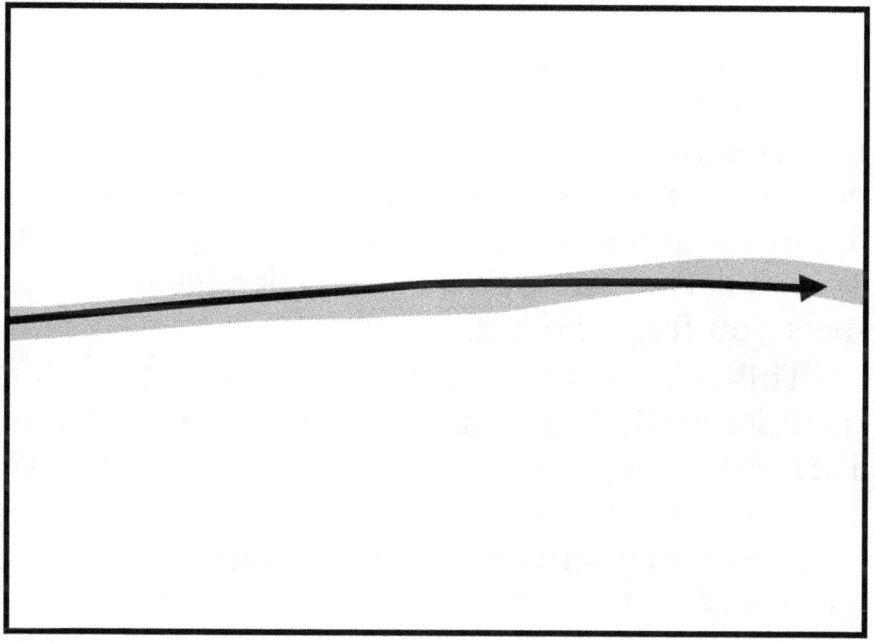

The incline that follows Turn 6 is the steepest uphill climb on the track. Even with 600 bhp you will be straining for more speed on this segment. You will be WOT as you take your straight driving line off the right edge track out from Turn 6 to a spot about one to one and a half car widths to the right of the visible left edge of the track surface as you begin the ascent.

Note the raised corner worker station to the left of the rumble stripes and before the hill crest. This worker will be critical to you for two signals. One will be the sound violation "meatball" flag. The second is to warn you of any impending trouble at the entry to the Corkscrew of Turn 8, as it is over a hill crest and not visible to you as you come WOT up the hill.

As you come up towards the top of the hill the track curves slightly left to right and pinches in towards you. The rate of ascent decreases and acceleration increases as you crest the hill. By following this straight line from the right edge at Turn 6 corner exit below, the track edge comes to meet you from the left.

This is Turn 7 and it really becomes an aiming point for setting up your entry to the Corkscrew of Turn 8-8A, as your left wheels cut along the edge of the rumble stripes.

Another opportunity to check your mirrors and gauges is up this hill.

If you have a modestly powered car and a high horsepower/high torque brute is on your tail, this is a good place to point them by, remembering to predictably stay with your driving line.

(**Beginners note**: Resist the temptation to pull over to the left edge of the track too soon after

TURN 7 - THE "RAHAL STRAIGHT"

exiting Turn 6. You will describe an "S" shape driving line which is geometrically too long.

Look to the left as you climb the hill for the potential of a meatball flag denoting sound violation or a problem in the Corkscrew Turn 8-8A which is blind to you from below during the hill ascent.

As you reach the "apex" of Turn 7, which is really just the extension of your straight approach up the hill where you get both of the left wheels on the edge of the stripes, you will be looking cross track to the right for your turn in to set up the entry and braking segment for the Corkscrew.)

Entry to Turn 8. *Manage your braking over the hill crest.*

Entry to Turn 8A. *Note alignment with oak tree trunk at turn in.*

Turn 8 - the "Corkscrew"

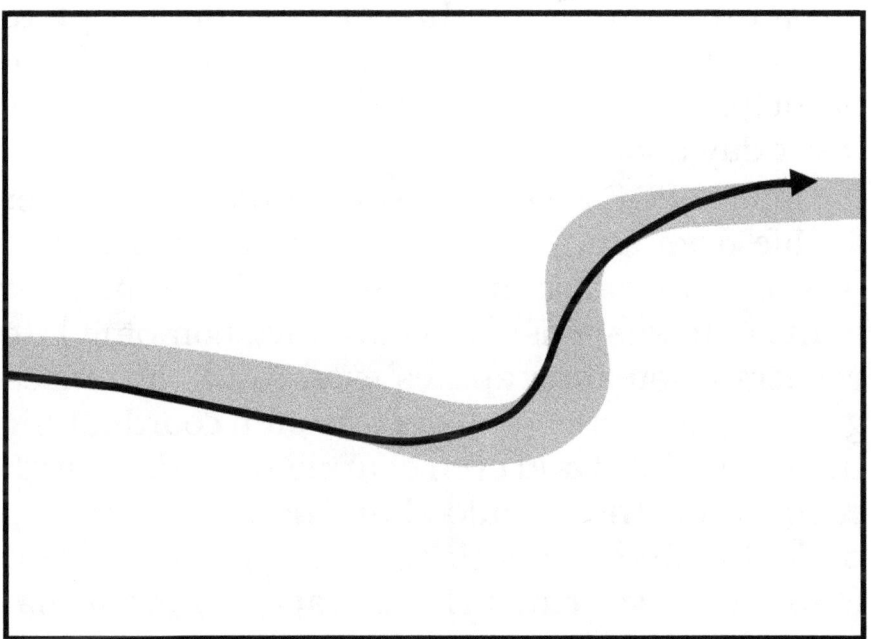

Now you begin your set up for Turn 9. That is correct, Turn 9.

What happened to Turn 8? The "Corkscrew" of Turn 8-8A is dramatic, and fun, but because it is a linked pair of the slowest corners on the track, it is a place to lose time, not gain it.

What you are looking for is the best corner exit speed you can safely manage from Turn 8A. That is your goal from the Corkscrew, not how fast you can buzz in there. Yes, track trivia buffs all remember what Alex Zanardi did by passing Bryan Herta in a Champ car to the inside of Turn 8 in the Corkscrew... but just forget about that when you are driving it yourself. Your odds of a successful outcome of trying that technique will be bettered by jumping from a plane without a parachute into a freshly plowed field, not to mention being summarily ejected from participation in the rest of the day's runs by the track day sponsor.

Most HPDE event sponsors would ban a driver for life from any future events for such a move. Any car to car contact is usually cause for immediate suspension, as are dive bombing into corners or stealing apexes even in the advanced groups. As event sponsors are often coordinating track schedules and even sharing track dates with each other, they would share news of your bad behavior, likely resulting in your permanent inability to ever run a HPDE track day event that any of them sponsor. It also assumes you successfully digested the torque wrench you were later force fed by the other drivers in the pit area.

Faster exit speed from Turn 8A is carried into entry and through the Rainey Curve of Turn 9 and steeply down the hill to Turn 10, so *that* is your focus.

TURN 8 - THE "CORKSCREW"

You take a slight turn in to the right from Turn 7, transition across the track from left to right, take the car to the crest of the hill with the right wheels on the edge of the rumble stripes, and initiate a two or possibly three gear drop under straight braking.

This section is blind as you come over the top and approach corner entry, and you want to finish your downshift and a portion of your straight braking as you crest the top of the climb. You may need to ease off the brakes as you crest, then reapply pressure right after settling, because the down force on the tires that aids in giving grip lessens when the car momentum is going slightly upward. The same brake pressure that was at ideal thresh hold limits just a few feet before can result in sudden locking up of the wheels, both front and rear, thus causing the tires to slide and with such loss of traction, skid through the upcoming corner entry. You cannot be WOT in most cars over the crest and still be able to slow the car adequately, so you have brake modulation challenge as you approach corner entry. If you watch experienced racers pushing the envelope of braking capacity in this corner, you will see a lot of squiggly fronts and rears as they fight to maintain full grip through this segment. You should not be pushing either yourself or the car that hard in this corner.

Stay along the right edge all the way to your late turn in point, and *resist the temptation to creep or crab your driving line over slightly to the left towards the corner.* You take the corner apex on Turn 8 slightly late, and when the nose of the car has rotated from right to left to where it is pointed at the middle trunk of the oak trees (there are presently three tree trunks, two closely together to the center left and one slightly more to the right... so take the right-most of the pair, or the middle of the three)... you quickly but smoothly unwind the steering fully, and as it returns to center steering squeeze throttle back on

The track surface is completely invisible at this moment of alignment and steering transition, because it drops away from you and is masked by the nose of the car. You cannot see the apex, or really any part of the track below you leading to Turn 8A. (The photo on page 80 shows the track surface and car below because the camera was mounted on the windshield above the driver eye level and about two and a half feet farther forward. For the driver in most street cars everything below the top of the wall in the photo is not visible at corner entry to Turn 8A.)

As the front of the car begins falling sharply away you smoothly initiate steering from the left to the right and continue the squeeze on throttle. The car should grip hard as your forward velocity is not great, weight is falling forward on the left front from the steep descent and turn to the right, and you track out briskly to the left edge. Be mindful of applying too much throttle after the corner apex as the weight shifts back to the rear during track out, and may then exceed the grip of your left front tire so that you push off track to the left.

It takes a little faith that the road in Turn 8A will in fact be there, as you briefly stare into space off the nose of the car at the top of Turn 8, but it always is.

Be looking for the track out point on the left edge ahead, not staring down off the nose looking for roadway as you fall down the slope, nor be fixated searching for the apex of Turn 8A, which is essentially invisible until you are right on top of it. Your driving line is determined by your steering input BEFORE you can see the apex of Turn 8A and is all based on memory and visual cues (the oak trees!). So focus on the track out point forward and to the left edge of the track, and use peripheral vision to mark the apex of Turn 8A.

If you drive your line off the nose of the car, you can find yourself looking up too late to avoid driving off track on the left at the track out point because the human reaction time is just too short. You have to be anticipating and inputting your driving commands before visual recognition of the traditional apex and track exit points can be made in this section.

Be careful to squeeze the power on gently and smoothly so that in your exuberance you do not break traction from the rear wheels and spin in the tight left to right downhill segment of Turn

8A. No jerky inputs with hands or feet. No ragged or violent steering. Take it slow into the top of the corner of Turn 8 and transition the weight to the right side and then back to the left side into Turn 8A smoothly.

(**Beginners note**: Watch the flag station on the left as you approach Turn 8, which is located ground level on the inside of the turn, and finish your straight braking before turn in, because if somebody has spun out at the bottom of Turn 8A, you will not see them on corner entry to Turn 8 and evasive maneuvers will probably be impossible to make.

The typical location of a spin out car is directly sideways or broadside in your driving line, just beyond the hill crest, out of your line of sight, with the driver below (and especially passenger if there is one) mouth agape, engine stalled, staring helplessly upwards at your approaching front bumper, descending towards them under acceleration throttle with its gleaming tow hook leading like the battering ram of a Roman trireme.

You have room to add a bit more brake at corner entry and to then safely maneuver around someone in that predicament if you are paying attention to the early warning the corner worker can give you. This corner worker is perhaps your best friend of the day, so pay close attention to him/her!)

Turn 9 - the "Rainey Curve"

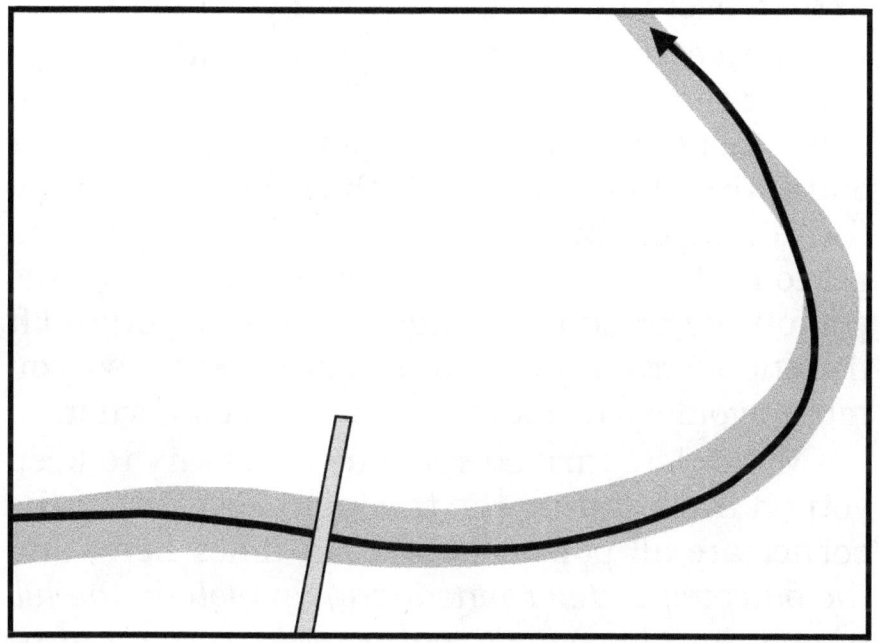

Approaching the left edge of the track out from Turn 8A note the corner worker's station for Turn 9 on the right edge. Aim right for it, having rolled on the power to full, and up shift to your next gear.

The track has rumble stripes on the right edge as you head towards the corner station, but before you get there apply a short braking segment straight towards the station to move some weight forward, then initiate your turn in, get the front right wheel to take a set, roll on power, and leave about one to as much as two car widths to the edge of the track surface. The pavement drops sharply downhill and acceleration is dramatic, almost like a looping roller coaster dive as it begins to turn over and down... but without the rails.

The correct driving line is essential as the camber early through mid corner helps to pull you down inside to the corner apex, again at the far end of the white curb inside the rumble stripes on the left edge. But the camber falls off after you get to mid track on the corner exit, and can slide you off the track to the right, requiring you to lift throttle or even give a touch of braking, so you must avoid early apexing this very fast corner.

Mid or late turn corrections necessary to keep you on track during the track out segment of the corner are all poison to fast lap times here, and *the outcome is determined way up high on the hill at your turn in commitment point for corner entry.*

Swivel your head far left as you finish your short braking touch at the top, and mark the corner apex that lies far below. You must "wait for it" before literally "diving" into the corner. As you confirm that you will not drift off right you can stay on throttle and use the gravity to pull you very fast downhill, possibly even making an up shift to the next gear. Make a cross track straight run at WOT from the right edge track out point to a target, the number 4 braking marker, and straighten along the left edge.

(**Beginners note**: The descent through Turn 9 can be startlingly fast, and the loss of camber helping you into the corner as you now exit at the right side of the track very disconcerting. Don't turn too quickly into the apex, but try to patiently *sweep* into it smoothly so you get a very wide line on entry and then shoot more straight down the track through the corner apex.

These few extra degrees of angle will keep the positive camber working longer for you and help you accelerate faster downhill. They also align you more directly down the hill and reduce your track out inertial energy towards the right edge of the surface.

The segment of track downhill appears long and a good place to execute a pass, but you should refrain from doing that unless given a point by very early and with plenty of room to get over to the left side, because all cars are accelerating fast here, and you do not want to be out of position for entry to Turn 10 by being anywhere other than on the far left edge of the track.

The speeds are so high on track out from Turn 9 relative to the distance in the straight which follows, that the pursuing car would have to be right on the tail of the pursued car going into and through the Rainey Curve, and that is a problematic position in non race conditions. If the car being passed does not voluntarily lift throttle to help the passing car get by following corner exit, there is a good chance that the braking point at Turn 10 for both cars will be reached before the passing car has fully merged back to the left edge driving line. And because there is an immediate cross track transition from right to left following corner exit, the possibility exists that the point by could be to either side of the pursued vehicle. Thus a second opportunity for a bad outcome is presented in this one section.

That will also make a safe entry to Turn 10 much slower for both cars. The passing car has a narrower radius arc turn and has to slow to keep from running off track, if the point by was to the right side, or the passing car has the faster driving line to the outside but may not have gained clearance before turn in relative to the passed car, and the passed car has to slow even more in either scenario to avoid running into the rear or rear quarter of the passing car.

Better most times to let the car pass occur between Turns 10 and 11, or the following front straight. Remember, if you are the pursuing car and you get the point by signal, it is your decision on whether to take the opportunity presented or not to take it, and it is your responsibility to do it safely if you do take it.)

Turn 10

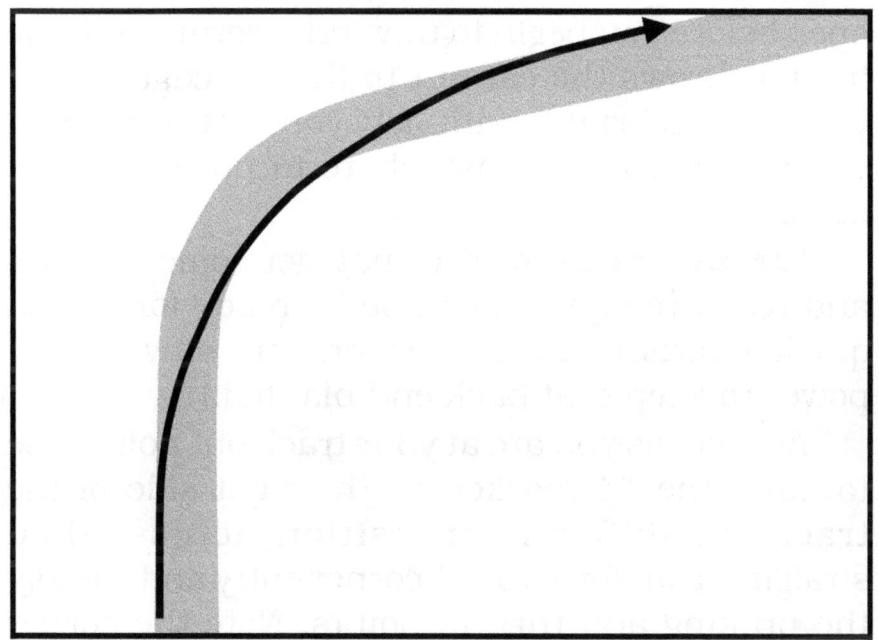

Properly aligned along the left edge, make a hard straight braking segment near the #3 marker, downshift, and make your turn in at the #1 marker.

Turn in to the late corner apex point of Turn 10 and roll on the power a bit early with the advantage of positive camber in the first half of the left to right corner. Note that with the camber working for you, it is possible to apex the corner a bit earlier, but how much really depends on the power you have and your suspension settings.

The track edge on the left comes up quickly as you exit the corner, and again the camber falls away in the second half of the corner, so to be safer try to stick with a later apex, hold on the steering lock just a touch longer through the corner apex before you begin to unwind steering, and the inertia throws the car out to the left edge. Once you get comfortable with how your car is reacting you may start to adjust where to put your apex mark.

(**Beginners note**: You may get some rotation and rear tire squeal here, so be ready for it with quick hands to counter steer, and stay on the power to keep that back end planted.)

As soon as you are at your track out point ease towards the #4 marker on the right side of the track, upshift and transition across, then straighten out for Turn 11 corner entry and identify the braking and turn in points. Note the corner worker station at the right side tower at the end of the straight. The k rail wall on the left blocks your vision of the track, so check for flags from the corner worker.

Turn 11

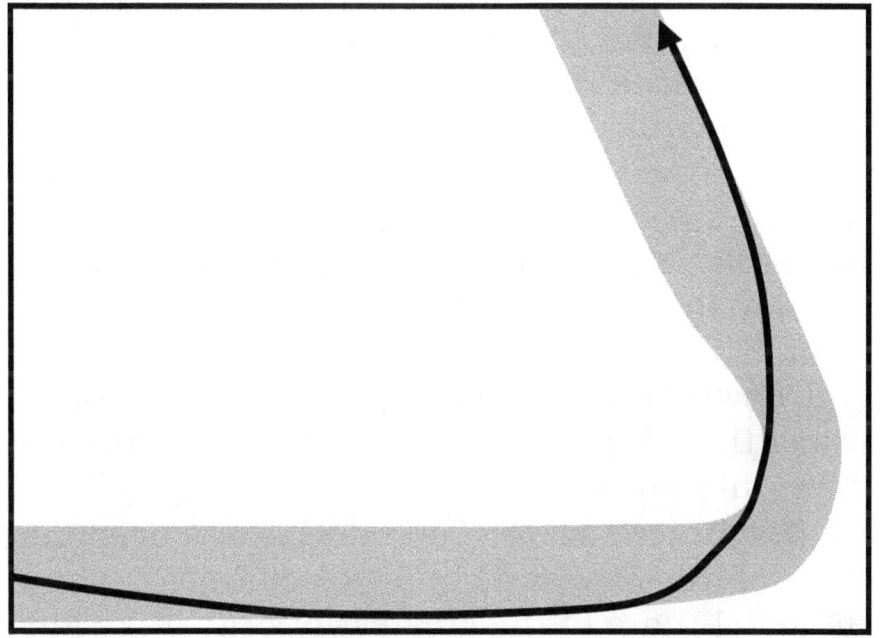

This final corner is tighter than it looks, more than 90 degrees, and feels as narrow as a supermarket aisle, so enter it more slowly than you might think you should.

There is a strip of artificial turf along the striped edge at the corner exit which possesses the surface adhesion qualities of leather dress shoes on hockey rink ice. This is followed by a gravel trap and a concrete wall. So don't early apex Turn 11.

Because this is one of the longest straights, the exit speed from the very slow Turn 11 is of high priority. Do not enter this corner too fast and thus sacrifice corner exit speed all the way down the front straight. Straight brake hard along the right edge of the track, downshift two gears in most cars, then take a *very late* apex on a very slow, flat corner. Put the front left wheels on top of the rumble stripes, add a touch of trail brake to help rotate the rear of the car a few degrees so you can get it pointed where you want to go, begin to unwind steering and only then get on throttle a tad earlier and harder, so that it will carry you all the way to the track edge, but not over it, on the right. The faster exit speed will be carried with you down the front straight, past start/finish under the bridge, up the hill, through Turn 1 and down into Turn 2.

(**Beginner's note**: You may have noticed that three of the slowest corners, specifically Turns 3, 8A and 11, are of the greatest priority at Laguna Seca because they lead to segments that are the longest straights or straights connected by a fast corner that can be negotiated almost like a straight in some cars. A fourth corner of critical importance is Turn 5, because in many cars it can lead to a WOT climb to the top of the course, so every fraction of a mph of additional corner exit speed is extended over that distance.)

Track Exit

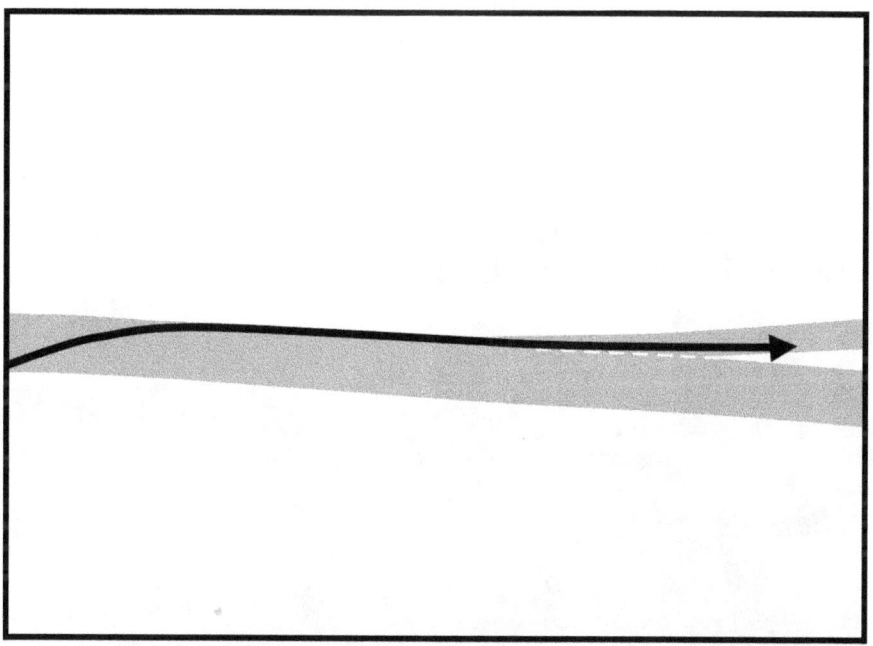

There are two exits typically used. The first exit is on the left following Turn 9 but before Turn 10, and leads down hill directly to the lower paddock area. The second and more commonly used exit is on the left after Turn 10 and before Turn 11.

Both exits allow the driver to take the corner preceding exit at full speed, track out and then get the left arm out and up to signal the intent to exit the track to the cars behind. Stay on speed so as not to slow the cars behind, but then as soon as you exit the track surface you must brake solidly to slow the car to a safe speed before turning into the hot pit lane or entering the paddock as is the case for the exit after Turn 9.

The exit after Turn 10 takes you parallel to the track, then a slow speed sharp left between a tire wall on the right and concrete k rail on the left, which leads to the hot pit run straight up alongside the front straight to the starter, or through a break in the wall and a gate on the left into the paddock about a third of the way up the straight and at the end of the garage building.

Track exit.

Distinguishing Characteristics

Where does one begin? This road course has many corners that the driver cannot see through, mandating careful continuous attention to corner station flag workers at the start/finish line, and Turns 2, 3, 4, 5, 6, 7, 8 and 11. Three hundred feet of elevation changes, corner camber changes in Turns 1, 2, 3, 5, 6, 8, 9, and 10, challenging braking segments before Turns 2, 5, 8, 10 and 11 and "steer with your feet" and counter steer corners in Turns 2, 4, 5, 8, 10 and 11, two high speed blind hill crests in Turns 1 and 7, left foot braking options in turns 3, 4, 6 and 9... the ultimate in unique compound turns with the legendary Corkscrew of Turn 8-8A, the heart in your throat approach downhill into and through the Andretti Hairpin, and the thrilling roller coaster dive into Turn 9. If you complain that this track only has ten real turns and is not technically complex enough... come *back and go a little bit faster next time.* The advanced driver will certainly find that the corner apex and driving line will vary for different power level cars, but also for driving styles, calling for skillful adjustment in how to approach and navigate them to extract best results.

Turn 9. *Note positive camber in mid corner, and flat camber at corner exit*

Conclusion

All of these characteristics and more add to the excitement and just pure joy of a day driving Laguna Seca Raceway. It is a road course that, if you are a performance car driver, you must find a way to get to and experience yourself. It is a wonderfully fun track to run in one of the most beautiful venues in all of motorsports.

Reflect for just a moment, that all of the driving decisions described above, and more, will transpire in a single lap, compressed into about one and three quarter minutes, as contrasted to the considerably longer time that it took you to read a summary description. And will be repeated ten to twelve times in a single session of HPDE driving, without pause or respite physically, mentally or emotionally. And you will have four, five or even six sessions available to you in a single day of driving.

Turn 10. *Note positive camber in early part of corner goes away quickly following corner apex.*

Turn 11. *Corner exit speed is priority as front straight beckons.*

Closing Note on Driving Lines

There is much more to determining the optimal driving line (and braking inception points, corner turn in points, corner apex points, track out points, etc.) than just an exercise in geometry on a flat road map. Because that is only the starting place for developing the "best" driving line for you.

Track conditions will influence your evaluation of the line to take. What is the weather? Is it cold or warm? Is it dry, humid or even wet? What is the condition of the surface in any given location of the track? Is the camber positive, negative or neutral? Is the surface ascending or descending?

The car you are driving will influence your evaluation of the line to take. What type of car are you driving, how heavy is it, what is the weight balance of the car, where are the drive wheels, what type of suspension (springs/dampers/control arms/camber adjustments/anti sway bars/strut towers/bushings), what type of tire and tire compound, inflation pressure, tire size, how much horsepower/torque, what type of slip differential, what type and size of brakes/brake fluid/pads do you have?

Who is driving will influence the evaluation of the line to take. What is your experience, what are your skill sets, how familiar are you with the particular track, what is your physical condition, are you mentally sharp and focused today?

Now add to this the fact that many of these factors are variables that change throughout the course of the day, indeed some of them through the course of a single session. Accordingly the purpose of the driving lines presented in this guide are to give a general orientation for you to become familiar with the track and then promptly develop your own before you begin to push your personal envelope that day. Obviously, novices should not be "pushing" anything other than the priority of having a fun safe day by staying well under the limits of performance for the track, the car, and themselves. This guide is not written to teach driving. There are many other excellent books that address technique, and excellent driving and racing schools. I encourage you to explore both to the fullest of your ability to do so, as they will enhance both your safety and enjoyment of high performance driving.

Track Checklist

Minimum Required of All Run Groups

- ☐ Helmet. Snell rated SA 2000 or better. Motorcycle helmets are not acceptable.
- ☐ Tech Inspection form
- ☐ Car Numbers – required on both sides of the car and rear, a minimum of eight inches high – this can be with blue painter's masking tape – any self adhering but removable and re usable numbers, vinyl or magnetic, must not peel off at high speed
- ☐ Tow hook installed (preferred) or tow point clearly established
- ☐ Long sleeve cotton shirt and full waist to ankle cotton pants (Cotton or Nomex clothing ONLY. No leather or synthetics allowed. This includes underwear).
- ☐ Closed toe shoes, preferably with a thinner sole for improved pedal feel, cotton socks
- ☐ Torque wrench, lug nut socket that fits your wheels
- ☐ Tire pressure gauge

Highly Recommended for Intermediate and Advanced Groups

- ☐ Driving Suit of not less than two layers, preferably three layers, fire resistant Nomex
- ☐ Race Driving gloves
- ☐ Race Driving shoes

- ❏ Nomex socks, undergarments, balaclava
- ❏ Face shield for helmet
- ❏ Fire Extinguisher, fixed within reach of seated and belted driver
- ❏ Neck brace, collar or Hans Device
- ❏ Racing seat or bucket
- ❏ Properly installed harness system of five points or more, three inch or more belt width.

Optional Supplies

For the Driver:

- ❏ Drinking water or electrolyte drinks. No alcohol drinks permitted on track site at any time. No smoking anywhere in the garage or pit areas.
- ❏ Hat - for Sun
- ❏ Sunglasses
- ❏ Sun Screen
- ❏ Folding chair
- ❏ EZ-UP Canopy
- ❏ Hand Soap/clean wipes
- ❏ Ice chest
- ❏ First aid kit
- ❏ Map/directions/phone number of hotel
- ❏ Map/directions/phone number of track
- ❏ Camera
- ❏ Camcorder/mount

For the Car:

- ❏ Extra Brake pads
- ❏ Brake fluid – one bottle
- ❏ Engine Oil – two quarts

TRACK CHECKLIST

- ❏ Power steering fluid – one bottle
- ❏ Coolant-Radiator- one gallon
- ❏ Distilled Water – Radiator- one gallon
- ❏ Duct tape – one roll
- ❏ Painter's tape – one roll
- ❏ Glass cleaner - You will kill some bugs on your way to the track. You may collect rubber streaks from "marbles" and more bugs on the track
- ❏ Brake Bleeder line and collector bottle
- ❏ Hose Clamps- assorted sizes
- ❏ Zip ties – one dozen
- ❏ Work gloves, heat resistant
- ❏ Jack – as light a weight yet strong as you can find
- ❏ Two foot long wood 2" X 4" stud
- ❏ Jack stands (2) minimum
- ❏ Jumper Cables or Jump starter box
- ❏ Service manual
- ❏ Other tools (sockets, wrenches, pliers, screwdrivers, allen keys...)
- ❏ Utility knife, multipurpose tool, scissors
- ❏ Grease
- ❏ Paper Towels – one roll
- ❏ Clean rags - six
- ❏ Trash bags - two
- ❏ Run Flat aerosol cans
- ❏ Tie Wraps
- ❏ Stopwatch
- ❏ Race tires and wheels, one set
- ❏ Spare tire
- ❏ Tire pyrometer
- ❏ Flashlight
- ❏ Funnel for oil
- ❏ Gloves – disposable

- ❏ Air compressor for tires
- ❏ Data logger
- ❏ Transponder
- ❏ Two way radio/walkie-talkie set
- ❏ Bucket
- ❏ Chamois
- ❏ Bug cleaner/degreaser
- ❏ Mild car soap
- ❏ Car sponge

Tech Inspection Form

Driver:_____ Date:_____

Make:_____Model:_____

Year:_____ Color:_____Stock or Modified:_____

Note: If you are self-teching your car, it is your obligation to physically check every item on this form. Do not assume your lugs are tight, re-torque them to make sure. This checklist is for your safety and the safety of the others on the track with you, and should not be dismissed as a formality. If the item is "good" mark with a check. If it is not, write "NO" and call it to the attention of the registrar, and support will be found to assist you to address the issue. After teching your car, you must sign the bottom of the form (in both places if you're self teching), which indicates that you have, in good faith, checked every item on this form. Please bring this form with you to the track, or you'll have to do a new tech at the track before you will be allowed on the track, possibly missing your first run group.

WHEEL and TIRES
Street Tires:
❏ More than 2/32" of tread?
Race Tires:
❏ Good condition/no cording?
❏ Cuts or other defects?
❏ All lugs present and torqued?
❏ Hub/Center-caps removed?

ENGINE
❏ Any fluid leaks?
❏ Wires/hoses secured ?
❏ Throttle return springs tight?
❏ Radiator overflow OK?
❏ Battery properly secured?
❏ Battery terminals covered
    (rubber boots / duct tape OK)?
❏ Fluid lines OK?

BRAKES
❏ Pedal pressure firm?
❏ Fluid level correct?
❏ Lines OK?
❏ Brakes lights working?
❏ Pads more than 5mm?
❏ Rotors OK (no cracks, etc.)?

STEERING & SUSPENSION
❏ Wheel bearings OK (no play)?
❏ Steering tight?

BODY
❏ Gas cap OK?
❏ Body panels secure?

SAFETY EQUIPMENT
❏ Helmet approved?
    (Snell 2000 or newer, M or SA)
❏ Seats secure?
❏ Long sleeve cotton shirt?
❏ Closed-toed shoes?
❏ Seatbelts properly installed?

APPROVED SEATBELTS
The following systems are approved:
(Please check one)
❏ OEM 3-Point
❏ 5 or 6-Point
4-Point*
*All 4-Point systems must pass
 fech at the event.
*4-Point Belts inspected by:_____

Note: Mark each line with a check (✓) if that item is OK; write "NO" if that item is not OK.

Print Name: _____ Signature: _____

Start/Finish. *Note concrete wall on left. Leave yourself a safe margin to avoid contact or evasive correction at more than 100 mph.*

Dedication

This book is dedicated to the many people that this adventure in high performance driving has brought me together with, past-present-future, and that I would never have otherwise met. The fraternity of drivers at HPDE has been steadfastly friendly and supportive in these early years, with helpful advice in learning courses and driving, shouldering jacks and pushing cars on and off trailers, even sharing parts and tools when necessary. All with a genuine shared enthusiasm for the sport, and a concern for the safety and well being of each other on and off the track. I hope with this effort to give back to our growing community a resource that will encourage safety, responsibility and development of skills so that all involved, both experienced and novice, will stay safe and well as they pursue their passion for driving.

Front straight. *It is the responsibility of the overtaking car to complete a safe pass. Keep a safe distance away. Once the overtaking car has moved off the driving line to pass, the car being passed may lift throttle slightly to facilitate a safer pass.*

Entry to Turn 6. *Note the corner worker tower on the right. Know the flags and pay attention to the corner workers, your best friends on the track.*

Acknowledgement

Many thanks to my wonderful family, whose patience, understanding and trust of dear old Dad were essential to allow him to take the time to pursue this adventure in learning high performance driving, building (and breaking) his car multiple times, and whose encouragement to write this book have made it possible. Thanks to my sons Eric and Matthew for attending racing school classes with me and to Matthew for the hours of editing this book, to my son Greg for being a good passenger and copilot at HPDE events at Laguna Seca, my son Alex for always being supportive of everything I did all the time, and my daughter Elizabeth and wife Valerie for indulging the expense and never making me feel rejected while steadfastly refusing to set foot in the race car. And for Valerie accepting that I will never ski with her on the black diamond mountain runs because I consider the sport too dangerous.

Photo courtesy of Sammy Davis Photography–Los Angeles, CA

About the Author

Edwin Reeser is just another one of the millions of motorsports enthusiasts, who devotes entirely too much time, energy and funds to the passion of high performance driving. You too will have reached this point when 1) you won't supersize your french fries order for a few additional pennies but think nothing of spending another $1,500 for a high flow exhaust, 2) accept the logic of the racer's adage "if you are under control you are not going fast enough", and 3) have no emotional reaction to substantial cosmetic or mechanical damage to your car, when you formerly would have had hysterical upset from a door ding, other than concern over how long will it take before you can get back on the track.

Other Race Track Attack Guides from Sericin Publishing released in 2010:

Willow Springs International Motorsports Park - "Big Willow" - Rosamond, California

Buttonwillow Raceway Park - Race #13 Clockwise - Buttonwillow, California

Auto Club Speedway - Auto Competition Course with "Roval" - Fontana, California

Reno Fernley Raceway Park - Configuration A - Fernley, Nevada

Thunderhill Raceway Park, Willows, California

Track guides in preparation for future release:

Sears Point Raceway, Sonoma, California

Las Vegas Motor Speedway, Las Vegas, Nevada

Spring Mountain Motor Sports Ranch, Pahrump, Nevada

Willow Springs International Motorsports Park - Streets of Willow, Rosamond, California

For more information go to:
www.RaceTrackGuides.com

www.ingramcontent.com/pod-product-compliance
Lightning Source LLC
Chambersburg PA
CBHW072200100426

42738CB00011BA/2481